802 GAY STREET
PORTSMOUTH, OHIO 45662
(740) 353-7655

Col 1:9-14

EVANGEL TEMPLE
ASSEMBLY OF GOD
802 OAK STREET
PORTSMOUTH, OHIO 45662
(740) 353-7695

The Heart-*Changer*

Marcia Shedroff

WestBow
PRESS

Copyright © 2012 by Marcia Shedroff.

All rights reserved. No part of this book may be used or reproduced by any means, graphic, electronic, or mechanical, including photocopying, recording, taping or by any information storage retrieval system without the written permission of the publisher except in the case of brief quotations embodied in critical articles and reviews.

All scripture quotations, unless otherwise indicated, are taken from the New King James Version®. Copyright © 1982 by Thomas Nelson, Inc. Used by permission. All rights reserved.

Scriptures quotations in Chapter 3 and from Psalm 119 and Matthew 6:22 in Chapter 4 are taken from the King James Version (New Testament with Psalms and Proverbs, Red-Letter Edition, published by World Bible Publishers).

All other Scripture quotations in Chapter 4 and those marked (NIV) are taken from the Holy Bible, New International Version®, NIV®. Copyright © 1973, 1978, 1984, 2011 by Biblica, Inc.™ Used by permission of Zondervan. All rights reserved worldwide. www.zondervan.com.

The "NIV" and "New International Version" are trademarks registered in the United States Patent and Trademark Office by Biblica, Inc.™

Scripture quotations marked NLT are taken from the Holy Bible, New Living Translation, copyright © 1996, 2004, 2007. Used by permission of Tyndale House Publishers, Inc., Carol Stream, Illinois 60188. All rights reserved.

Scripture quotations marked TLB are taken from The Living Bible copyright © 1971. Used by permission of Tyndale House Publishers, Inc., Carol Stream, Illinois 60188. All rights reserved.

WestBow Press books may be ordered through booksellers or by contacting:

WestBow Press
A Division of Thomas Nelson
1663 Liberty Drive
Bloomington, IN 47403
www.westbowpress.com
1-(866) 928-1240

Because of the dynamic nature of the Internet, any web addresses or links contained in this book may have changed since publication and may no longer be valid. The views expressed in this work are solely those of the author and do not necessarily reflect the views of the publisher, and the publisher hereby disclaims any responsibility for them.

Cover photograph by Alice Baker. Stained-glass artwork by Gwyn L. Ditmars. Photo used by permission of both.

ISBN: 978-1-4497-3683-5 (sc)
ISBN: 978-1-4497-3684-2 (hc)
ISBN: 978-1-4497-3682-8 (e)
Library of Congress Control Number: 2012900468
Printed in the United States of America

WestBow Press rev. date: 3/23/2012

This book is in loving memory of Shirley. Thank you, Emily, Alice, Conni, Pamela, Madeline, Trena, Jo Ann, Laura, and Corinne for reading the manuscripts and making helpful suggestions.
To all my family: I love you.

Thus says the LORD:
    "Cursed is the man who trusts in man
    And makes flesh his strength,
    Whose heart departs from the LORD.
    For he shall be like a shrub in the desert,
    And shall not see when good comes,
    But shall inhabit the parched places in the wilderness,
    In a salt land which is not inhabited.

    "Blessed is the man who trusts in the LORD,
    And whose hope is the LORD.
    For he shall be like a tree planted by the waters,
    Which spreads out its roots by the river,
    And will not fear when heat comes;
    But its leaf will be green,
    And will not be anxious in the year of drought,
    Nor will cease from yielding fruit.

        "The heart is deceitful above all things,
        And desperately wicked;
        Who can know it?
            I, the LORD, search the heart,
            I test the mind,
            Even to give every man
            according to his ways,
            According to the fruit of his doings."

    Heal me, O LORD, and I shall be healed;
    Save me, and I shall be saved,
        For You are my praise.
        Jeremiah 17:5-10, 14

Introduction

~ ~ ~

On January 26, 1996, at the age of thirty-eight, I left my southern Ohio law practice, said goodbye to family and friends, and moved to California—to live behind steel-barred gates, locked away from the world. I lived there for nineteen months, with about one hundred other women of all ages, under many rules and restrictions on every facet of life. I was constantly under supervision, and even the most personal aspects of my life were monitored. Private moments were rare, and then I had to report not only what I had done, but also what I had thought and felt.

No, I wasn't in a prison, at least outwardly. I had voluntarily boarded the airplane that took me there and had willingly, even enthusiastically, entered this place of confinement. I could have packed up and left at any time during those nineteen months, but I didn't want to. I didn't realize it at the time, but the steel-barred gates were an outward symbol of my own inner prison. I thought I was free, but my heart, mind, and soul were anything but free.

What was this place? It was an "ashram," which means "house" in Sanskrit. But it was not just any house or home. It was like a monastery, or a convent, and I went there to become a monastic disciple, a nun—to devote my life to the teachings of a guru from India. I had never met him in person. In fact, he was dead. He had come to the United States in 1925 and spent several years gathering followers from all over the country by performing miraculous signs. He established a religious organization to spread his teachings. Then he died in 1952. This guru—or rather, his spirit—had entered my life in seemingly miraculous ways, and I had been all too willing to let him in.

The Heart-Changer

Why would a reasonably intelligent, educated, responsible woman, who had attended church every Sunday of her childhood, leave her career and loved ones to follow a dead guru and become a nun in a religion she had learned about less than two years before? What was so captivating? So convincing? What provided an escape from those steel-barred gates? And, more importantly, what—or who—provided an escape from the inner prison that had held her captive?

In the following pages, I'll tell you the story that answers these questions. My purpose isn't simply to tell you about me. I'm writing because, though my story may seem strange in the details, it may help you find answers to questions you have about your own life.

My decision in 1996 to go to the ashram revealed my beliefs at the time—beliefs about God, about myself, and about life—beliefs that are fairly common today. The story of my captivation tells much about God's enemy and the enemy of our souls, who has invaded all of our lives, whether we realize it or not. But the story of my rescue tells of the power and mercy of the true and living God. Only by His grace am I alive to tell this story. It's my prayer that you will find the freedom you long for deep in your heart.

Chapter One

~ ~ ~

The "Chela Incident"

I could say that it all began on a day in early April 1994, a day that came completely without warning as to its significance.

For several weeks prior, I had worked as an interim director at the local women's shelter. By profession, I was an attorney, but I'd been unable to work for two years because of the devastating symptoms of chronic fatigue syndrome. For months after a physical collapse in the spring of 1992, I had lain in my apartment, watching the shadows move along the wall throughout the day, day after day. I couldn't do much physically, but I determined to use the time to get to the bottom of my lifelong problems—bitter anger, depression, and hopelessness. When I regained enough strength to make trips to the library, I read every self-help book that looked somewhat promising. I wanted desperately to change, and I was willing to try anything. I was tired of the bitterness oozing out of me every time I felt provoked. I was weary of the nasty defense mechanisms that were so deeply entrenched in my personality. I put all my precious energy into trying to change myself, and I actually thought it was working. As I read the books and sincerely took in all they had to offer, I thought I was becoming a kind, loving person. Gradually my physical strength increased. When the opportunity came to fill in at the shelter, I hoped my time as interim director would be my re-entrance into the world as the new me, completely changed. But even on my first day at the shelter, within just two hours of dealing with the people and pressures, the old nastiness seeped out of my heart and into my words and behavior all over again. I was as mean and contentious as ever. Each day I felt defeated, and at the end of my term as interim director, I was emotionally exhausted. I was glad it was over, but so disappointed in myself.

This particular morning in April was the first day after the new director had assumed her duties. About 4:00 a.m., I awoke to heavy, thunderous thoughts rumbling through my mind: "What a failure! You've tried to change, but proven you can't, so you may as well give up. You don't even deserve to live! You're a waste! Who could ever love you?" After thirty-six years of emotional defeat, these thoughts were familiar to me, but they still felt like daggers through my heart. Turning to the only hope I had at the time, I reached for the umpteenth self-help book I had checked out from the library, yet another book that promised I could change. Trying desperately to get a grasp on my thoughts and find relief from an excruciatingly intense migraine, I began to meditate as I had been taught by one of the doctors who had treated me for chronic fatigue syndrome. He had taught me the simple technique of "following my breath" to manage pain and anxiety. As I calmed down a little, I pondered the self-help information I had just read and related it to my experiences at the shelter, facing the question that had been uppermost in my mind and heart for years: "How do I change myself?"

Suddenly, a bit of insight penetrated the pain, and I wrote in my journal: "I have pin-pointed my problem—what's making me unhappy and sick. It's judgment. I am constantly judging other people. I don't always behave badly toward them in a grossly violent way. In fact, I manage to be outwardly calm in many situations. But on the inside, I seethe with anger and condemn people when they are hurting me."

As a flood of unpleasant memories played on the screen of my mind, I paused at an incident years before in law school when I'd overheard classmates criticizing and demeaning me behind my back because of my Appalachian background and mannerisms. Their comments had left me emotionally paralyzed, stewing for

Chapter One

days in a poisonous concoction of self-pity, self-loathing, and anger—until I realized I could just forgive them. And when I forgave them, I felt better. I actually felt lighter.

As this memory replayed, I wondered why this lesson—that I could feel better by forgiving others—had never really become a part of me. I had forgiven my classmates back then in this one isolated incident, but my life as a whole was characterized by deep bitterness and lack of forgiveness, going back to childhood. Why had I not learned to forgive? The answer seemed obvious. I had grown up in an environment where being unforgiving was as basic as breathing. Bitterness and resentment had been "normal" to me. And there had simply been too much pain in my life—too much misery in the past and a seemingly endless onslaught of new pain as life unfolded.

But on this particular morning, I concluded that I must learn to forgive. I wrote in my journal, "The only way I will ever be happy—to be able to give and receive love—is to learn how to forgive." This fresh new idea produced a small spark of hope, and the throbbing in my head eased slightly.

I put down my journal and purposed in my heart that I would begin to seek the one way I'd abandoned long ago, the only way I'd ever heard of that even spoke of forgiveness—the way of Jesus. But then I pictured myself trying to find the Bible I'd packed away in a box and carried from apartment to apartment for years. I felt the resistance and inertia from the years in which I'd turned away from anything that looked or sounded like Christianity. My attitude toward Christianity could be summed up as, "tried it; doesn't work." Besides, it was still very early in the morning, and I felt that I should just rest my aching head and body for a little while. So I fell asleep.

When I awoke a couple of hours later, I felt better—and at that point, how I felt mattered most. I remembered my earlier resolve to seek out the way of forgiveness. The strong opposition in my heart to the very idea of opening a Bible outweighed my

The Heart-*Changer*

earlier motivation. My enthusiasm for reaching out to Jesus faded as my headache and anxiety diminished.

Instead, I decided to meditate more consistently. After all, I reasoned, meditation had been the only thing I could count on to calm me, although I had really only dabbled at it during the two years of my illness. Occasionally, I had "followed my breath," and at times I'd used some guided Buddhist and Taoist meditations on tapes from mail order catalogs. But my efforts had been hit or miss. This day, I resolved, would be the day that I started a consistent meditation practice.

So, I dove in. I decided that since my thoughts had raced so much that morning, perhaps transcendental meditation would be good for me. Although I'd never practiced transcendental meditation, I had read a little about it. As I settled in to meditate I thought, "Well, if I'm going to do TM, I'll need a mantra. If I had a mantra, what would it be?" Instantly, with no further thought or effort, the syllables "chay-lah" came into my mind. I used these syllables as my mantra and had a nice meditation. In fact, it was so nice and calming that I continued to use this mantra in a walking meditation outdoors. I even sang it to myself as I fixed lunch.

I had just received in the mail, on a free-trial basis, a set of tapes on meditation and yoga, so as I was eating my lunch and tidying my apartment, I started to listen. Everything on the tapes about yoga was new and unfamiliar to me. Born and raised in southern Ohio, and not being all that outgoing, I had not encountered anything quite like this. My doctor had been the only person with whom I'd ever discussed meditation in depth, but that was entirely different, like discussing a prescription. I listened to the tapes with curiosity borne of my earlier resolution to meditate consistently, but also with a little uncertainty. All this talk of yoga, gurus and such seemed so foreign.

My interest was suddenly aroused when the speaker began teaching about "the relationship between the guru and the chela"—pronounced "chay-lah."

Chapter One

"Hey, that's my mantra!" I thought as I stood up from dusting a table. And in the instant this thought went through my mind, as I stood there in the sunlight pouring through the window of my apartment, I immediately felt a presence with me. It was invisible, but it was tangible, inwardly. It was unlike anything I'd ever felt before. I knew I was not alone, but I had no idea what, or who, was with me. I had no idea what all this meant.

I backed up the tape to listen again and discovered that a *chela* is a follower, or disciple. Somehow this knowledge was exciting to me, but for a reason I couldn't yet articulate.

During the next weeks, as I continued to meditate, I had experiences that were amazing and perplexing, but, at the same time, intoxicating. I did nothing to bring these experiences on. I wouldn't have known how. They were involuntary, so to speak. But they were so pleasant—no, blissful!—that I didn't want them to stop.

On one occasion soon after the chela incident, as I was following my breath I felt an energy go from the base of my spine, up through my spine, into my brain, and beyond—to where I was not sure. It was as if I were in an ocean of sweet, warm, honey-like bliss. It was so wonderful that I couldn't take it for very long. I didn't know what made the experience end, but when it did I couldn't simply remain inside and go about mundane household activities. I went out into the sunlight and walked my daily route, although this day things were very different. I looked up at the trees, and I could "see through" them. I could see, or perceive, that they were projections of light. The bliss continued in this way, in that my perceptions were in some way heightened.

Soon after, on another day while I was meditating, my consciousness lifted out of my body. I looked down, first, on my apartment building; then, the surrounding neighborhood; then, the county; then, the state; then, the hemisphere; then, the world, as if I was suspended above it. Was it real or just my imagination?

I had no idea why these experiences were coming to me, but for weeks prior, a word had been recurring in my thoughts: "massage." With these new experiences in meditation, and considering the chela incident, I began to wonder whether there was some connection between all of this and the recurring word, "massage," as strange as that seemed. I thought perhaps I should get my first massage.

There were only two massage therapists listed in the phone book, so I chose the one closer to me. I was a little nervous, but within just a couple of minutes, the massage therapist and I were discussing "spiritual" matters. She explained her interest in psychic phenomena. Even after the massage, we continued to chat. Eventually, I felt I could trust her enough to tell her about the experiences I'd been having in meditation. She felt there was something significant going on, but she didn't know what it was, so she referred me to an actual psychic.

The thought of going to a psychic was at first too much for me. After all, I was really meditating just to feel better. Yes, the strange experiences in the previous weeks had spurred questions about supernatural things, but going to a psychic would be going too far, I thought. But after a week or two of mental debate, the lure of those blissful experiences was something I could not resist. I had to know what was going on. I had lived a lifetime of depression, pain, and hopelessness—but now bliss! I had to search it out. So, I called the psychic for an appointment.

Ironically, the psychic lived with her husband and family in a house about a hundred yards away from the church I'd attended as a child. Their apparent normalcy put me at ease. Yet she and her husband told me many things about myself they couldn't possibly have known by natural means, such as details of my health history, just from holding my watch. With each accurate proclamation, they gained more of my trust.

In the final part of the session I was alone with the psychic. She said she could see certain entities in the spirit realm that were near me, one of whom was a man with long, dark, wavy

Chapter One

hair. I immediately thought of my deceased husband, because I'd seen a picture of him as a teenager with beautiful long, wavy hair, but the psychic said she didn't think it was my husband. When I told her about my recent experiences in meditation, she matter-of-factly told me that I had a "master" and that he was communicating with me telepathically. I laughed out loud, then realized she was serious. The import of her words dawned on me. I asked if I would meet this master, and she said I definitely would and that I wouldn't have to travel over water to do it.

I left her presence feeling both elated and frightened. It was exhilarating to think that I had a master who had somehow entered my life and was communicating with me. "To make this effort, my master must truly care about me," I thought. "The blissful experiences must be leading to something great!" But it was also a bit frightening, because deep inside something felt dark and foreboding. I ignored these negative feelings. All that mattered was the bliss—and now the possibility that I belonged to someone.

I had to find out who this master was. For about a month, as I wondered how I would ever find him, things got worse. I felt no peace, and the pain in my body made me miserable. I was getting discouraged. One day while driving, I thought, "I may as well give up. I'll never find my master in this one-horse town." But remembering the bliss again, I thought, "No, I can't give up." Just then, as I was driving past the library, something urged me to stop there. I went inside and somehow felt led to the magazine rack, directly to a particular magazine. I opened it and saw a picture of the man with long, dark, wavy hair. His eyes captivated me. I seemed to "fall into" them. It was the guru. My life was about to change.

Experiencing Was Believing

I eagerly read the entire magazine. It was dedicated to this man, the master, the guru, and it was published by the organization he had founded. I had to know more! So I wrote to the organization, telling of my experiences in meditation, and of the chela incident, and asked to be put on their mailing list for correspondence lessons. Within a couple of weeks, I received the first package of literature. In addition to an explanation of their organization, they sent a pamphlet entitled "The Guru-Disciple Relationship." When I read it, any remaining doubts about what the psychic had told me vanished. I accepted the fact that this guru, even though dead, was my master. He was real to me. His presence was with me throughout my days and activities. I asked him questions, and he answered in various ways.

But I told no one. I kept it all secret. Who among my family or acquaintances would ever understand?

As the correspondence lessons arrived in their bi-weekly segments, I became even more convinced that I had found my true guru. He had written all the lessons between 1925 and 1952, yet the third lesson described in precise detail the experience I'd had in meditation a week or so after the chela incident—when my consciousness rose up and was suspended over the earth. "If I had the experience weeks ago, and now this lesson describes it, then all this must be true," I reasoned. I wanted it to be true.

The first twenty lessons or so contained material with which I could heartily agree, as much of it resonated with my Judeo-Christian background. The guru quoted from the Bible frequently, and the gist of these lessons was love, kindness, forgiveness, determination—topics with which anyone would be hard-pressed to disagree. The only new ideas in these lessons were the teachings about Jesus Himself. But I was ready to believe anything the guru had written.

He taught that Jesus was just one of six gurus we chelas would revere. Jesus had come to earth not to be a Savior in the sense Christianity teaches, but to reveal the truth of kriya (pronounced "kree-yuh") yoga—a kind of meditation the guru promised would lead to God. I read that Jesus had come up through the ranks of many incarnations, just as any other human

Chapter One

being would do; and largely because He had practiced kriya yoga, He had become an avatar—an enlightened one who had achieved "Christ-consciousness." Jesus had achieved this "self-realization," then voluntarily returned to earth for the benefit of mankind—not the forgiveness of sins, but rather the spreading of kriya yoga. Jesus bore some of the bad karma of His immediate disciples, just as the other gurus had done for theirs and as my guru would do for me, but He did not bear the sins of the world, the guru taught. Even though these lessons completely redefined Jesus, they incorporated the moral values of traditional Christianity. Because of the moral virtue espoused in the lessons, as well as the experiences I'd had in meditation, I was not the least bit shocked or offended by the guru's teachings about Jesus. In fact, my reaction was elation that, at last, I was learning the truth. To me, these teachings had been validated by their description of my previous experiences in meditation, and I was completely ready to believe this redefinition of Jesus. In my pride, I fancied that I was one of the chosen few in the whole world to be privy to the "real truth."

Soon the lessons weren't enough for me, so I ordered the guru's books. His autobiography was not merely the story of his life, but rather a thorough indoctrination into his teachings. I devoured it. And as other books, tapes, and music recordings arrived in the mail, I became more and more established in this new life, although it was a solitary life for me.

By the fall of 1994, my physical strength had returned so that I could work full time. I was amazed and delighted at this "healing," and I gave credit to the guru's meditation techniques and healing affirmations. I was ever more confident that the guru's teachings were true.

Mostly, I was guided by the feelings of bliss, love, and joy, which were new to me. My attitude had completely changed. I no longer felt hopeless. I felt loved. I devoted myself to the guru-disciple relationship. Although the guru was invisible to me, his presence was real. The bliss was a respite from the heartache and pain, the depression and hopelessness, I had always felt. And I deserved this respite. The lessons and books were teaching me that only a person who had attained a high level of spiritual growth in previous incarnations could have the kinds of experiences I was having. With this information, my past in this life made a little more sense. In all my prior misery, I had burned up the bad karma necessary to return to the guru, and my spiritual advancement would be even greater from this point on. Although I was trying to cultivate humility as a spiritual virtue, in my heart I believed that "it was due time" that all this good was happening to me.

Throughout my life I'd occasionally read small, isolated portions of the Bible. It was the same with the guru's teachings. He chose isolated verses from here and there, and he taught that all of these verses in some way or another referred to kriya yoga, an esoteric and highly secretive meditation practice, the particulars of which were kept from the chela until completion of at least one year's study of the guru's lessons. Being biblically ignorant for the most part, I readily believed the guru's claims about Jesus and the Bible.

Soon I acquired and framed a small cardboard "travel altar" on which the pictures of all six gurus were displayed. In the center were Jesus Christ and Krishna—both avatars who had attained "Christ-consciousness," according to the guru. Every day I sat for hours in front of this altar while meditating. I believed it was possible for me to attain Christ-consciousness through devoted practice of kriya yoga and right living. I wanted "self-realization."

Further, I had learned that there was a monastic order of monks and nuns who lived in solitude at the organization's headquarters, or ashram. I wanted nothing more than to devote my whole life to the pursuit of God—at least the concept of God I then had. If following the guru would lead to self-realization and God, then surely following more intensely as a monastic disciple would obtain quicker results. I determined that I would

Chapter One

practice the guru's teachings for the required year, then attempt to enter the ashram as a nun.

It became important to me to meet other devotees of the guru, and in the fall of 1994 I flew to Washington, D. C., for a weekend seminar. Special little things happened throughout the trip that convinced me the guru was with me all the way. The other devotees gave me special attention and said very kind things to me. Some even gave me flowers and gifts. I felt like Cinderella. Most importantly, I met with the monk who was giving the seminar, and I told him of some of my experiences in meditation. I just needed to hear him say that I really belonged to the guru. The monk assured me with all confidence that I was, indeed, a disciple of the guru. In the afternoon session after I'd met with him, the monk spoke on a passage from the Bible—the kingdom of God is like a treasure buried in a field, so valuable that once you've found it you sell everything you own just to buy that field. This was exactly how I felt! Nothing in my life was too much to give up for all the guru had done and would do for me, I thought. I was determined to follow the guru with every ounce of my being.

During the following months, I meditated at least an hour each morning and evening and came home for lunch to listen to the guru's teaching tapes. On weekends my meditation sessions increased to three hours. My peers in the legal profession began to comment on the changes in me—my calmness and peace—much to my inward delight. After all, this change was not without great effort on my part. The guru taught that the true savior of mankind was a "progressive dynamic will," a will that gained strength each day by kriya yoga and right living. I wanted such a will. It was up to me to rid myself of everything that hindered my spiritual progress, so I had to make every effort, every day.

Life still had its difficulties, but I was undaunted. The guru was with me. He showed me practical things, and sometimes even helped me with legal research. He showed me things that were going to happen in the future so that I could prepare. At

The Heart-*Changer*

times, he made me aware of other people's thoughts—a great advantage for a lawyer! The guru seemed like a constant supplier of happiness.

For an entire year, I looked forward to the world-wide convocation of the guru's devotees and saved money for the trip to Los Angeles in August 1995. The convocation would be my opportunity not only to be among the most dedicated devotees in the world, but also to meet with the nun's entrance committee on my application to enter the ashram.

The convocation proved to be as wonderful as I thought it would be. With other devotees I took day trips to various locations and shrines in southern California. One of these trips was to the Forest Lawn Cemetery, where the guru's body lies in a mausoleum. Small groups of devotees sat in chairs in front of his crypt to meditate for a few minutes. Then we were to approach the crypt one by one and bow Indian-style with our hands held together in obeisance, in a "pranam." When it was my turn, I bowed in deep adoration and put my forehead lightly on the crypt. A shock of energy entered my body, and the sound of "om" resonated in my consciousness. I felt overwhelming devotion. This experience was typical of each day of convocation for me—one special time after another.

My first interview with the nun's entrance committee happened mid-week in the convocation. The committee consisted of three nuns who had attained the highest "rank" in the order. It became pertinent to tell them of my experiences in meditation from the beginning, and I described the one that had occurred just shortly after the chela incident—the one in which the energy went from the base of my spine, up through my spine, into my brain, and out into bliss. Upon hearing this, the nuns immediately put my name on the schedule for the kriya yoga initiation ceremony the next day, even though I had not finished the lessons required to qualify. Who was I to argue? I was thrilled!

Because I hadn't yet received the correspondence lessons on kriya yoga practice, I didn't know exactly what to expect. From the guru's description in his autobiography, I knew kriya had something to do with the subtle energies of the body, but I knew none of the details. Nevertheless, even without this knowledge, I was more than willing to undergo the initiation ceremony.

It took place mostly in the dark, literally without lights, in the large ballroom of the hotel. We chanted songs and heard stories of the guru from one of the monks who had been with him in person. We brought the guru gifts of fruit and flowers, as we were assured that he was there in spirit. The culmination of the initiation ceremony was when each of us received a touch on the forehead by a monk who was "spiritually advanced" in kriya yoga meditation. At that moment, each chela confirmed and cemented his or her relationship with the guru. When the monk touched my forehead to place the red mark there, once again, as at the guru's crypt, I heard the "om" and felt overwhelming devotion.

Just after the ceremony I went to an instructional meeting to review the basics of the kriya yoga technique. There I understood why the nuns had decided to allow me to receive the initiation early. The bliss experience was the ultimate goal of kriya yoga! I realized that I had received the bliss of *samadhi*, or "oneness with God," before I even knew what it was. My joy was practically uncontainable. I believed what the guru had taught—that the bliss in meditation *was* God—and I was getting close! I would practice kriya more and more until I could sustain that bliss.

I had all the "proof" I needed. For me, experiencing was believing. I thought I had found truth at last, and from this truth my life would finally have meaning.

It would take two years before I would begin to realize my problem: I was my own judge of truth, and my own experiences were the sole basis for my judgment. I was greatly deceived.

Chapter Two

~ ~ ~

Seeds of Deception

I *could* say it all began that day in April 1994, but actually I had begun to fall deeply into deception much, much earlier than that. Seeds of deception had been sown in the ground of my heart even from experiences and decisions early in childhood. Long before the chela incident, I had believed lies that affected the deepest part of me—lies about myself, about life, and about God. In fact, it's possible to trace my decision to go to the ashram back through a lengthy line of lies. I'll start at the beginning.

I was my parents' third living child. They had been traumatized by the stillbirth of a son eighteen months before my birth. Then, early in infancy, because of a defect in my digestive tract, I became severely dehydrated and would have died but for an emergency surgery. All this stress proved to be too much for my parents' already-strained relationship. From my earliest memories, my family's life was full of strife, contention, and bitterness. Things went better if I didn't make childish mistakes, so I learned to try my very best at all times. Tempers ran hot, and I heard words that left deep scars. "You've ruined my life! I wish you'd never been born!" These were as painful as physical blows, perhaps even more so. I was too young to realize these words came in moments of frustration and anger, and not because of anything I'd done; so, I internalized them and accepted them as true.

Filled with a deep sense of rejection, I succumbed to depression. It became normal to me. I felt guilty and ashamed

The Heart-*Changer*

for being alive, so it's not surprising that I believed my life had no value.

I couldn't sleep, so I'd stare into the night sky through my bedroom window, my heart aching for something I didn't know how to express. At church I had heard about God, but it never occurred to me that He could possibly love or want me. I felt as disconnected from and unwanted by God as I did my family. I'd learned that the safest way to live was to keep quiet and not ask for anything, and I related to God in the same way. It was the only way I knew. My heart longed for more, but it wasn't my place to ask God for whatever it was. The only times I remember praying were on those nights, looking up into the sky, when I'd ask God just to let me die.

My feelings were confused and contradictory. I wanted love and acceptance from my family, but sometimes found myself hating them, resulting in more guilt. Even though I hated myself deeply just for living, I grew to love myself in a very destructive way—through self-pity. From an early age, I began refusing to feel my real emotions; but when the emotional pain welled up too strongly to be suppressed, self-pity was my "medication." I didn't realize what I was doing, but when I felt overwhelmed by rejection or loneliness, I could soothe myself in this way. Somehow feeling sorry for myself took the edge off the pain, and, in a way, I became addicted to it.

I now know that self-pity was a cheap counterfeit for the love I really wanted. It was only the first of many counterfeits I would embrace in life. The deep root of rejection and bitterness was like an impenetrable wall around my heart. I simply could not comprehend love.

When I was five or six, an evangelist came to conduct a revival at our church. I remember that during one of the services, many people went to the altar weeping. I had little idea what it was about, but I had enough guilt feelings to make me mournful as well. I found myself sitting alone in the pew. The organist caught my attention and asked, "Do you want to go up there, too?" I nodded my head. She motioned for me to go, and I joined my father at the altar. He asked if I believed that Jesus died for my sins. I nodded. He asked if I believed that Jesus rose from the dead. I nodded again.

I had no reason to doubt that Jesus died for my sins or that He rose from the dead, but in my young heart, it just made me feel more guilty—I had apparently ruined Jesus' life as well. I believed the facts about Jesus but had no idea what it all meant for me.

When I was about nine, a missionary who had served in Java, Indonesia, spoke at our church. His stories fascinated me, and I began to imagine myself as a missionary in a faraway land. Although I never told anyone in my family, I decided that I would be a missionary. This aspiration had more to do with my desire to escape home than it did devotion to God. Although I always tried to be very good, the thought of God ever actually loving me was—well, unthinkable.

I spent a lot of time alone—reading, studying, ruminating—and by the time I was about eleven, I was bored with my own school books. I borrowed some of my older sister's textbooks from her college geology and paleontology classes and learned of Darwin's theory of evolution. This new information shook my worldview. God had seemed distant and impersonal, but I had had no reason to doubt what I'd heard from the Bible—that there was a God who created everything, including me. Doubts entered my mind, and these led to a fear deeper than I could fathom. Not only was my individual life a mistake, but all of human life was a mistake—a random, meaningless event in a random, meaningless universe. There was no one with whom I could discuss my feelings. I wasn't even capable of articulating my confusion. Something in me would not let me accept the Bible or evolution completely, so I blended them. My eleven-year-old mind came up with the hybrid belief that God created the earth, the planets and the stars, but that from His distance He used evolution to create life forms and to shape them into the way they are today. God was even less interested in me than I had originally thought!

My depression took on a life of its own, and every experience and observation seemed to feed it. I watched as adults went to jobs they didn't enjoy and come home to a life they didn't enjoy, and I wondered why people bothered to go on living. Each August we went to the county fair, which was supposed to be the major yearly "fun event" in our lives, but as I walked through the fairgrounds I could barely hold back tears of futility and disgust. All I could see were poor, desperate people trying to fill up the profound emptiness of life with cheap carnival rides and worthless trinkets. The meaninglessness of life was a constant ache in my chest.

But eventually my pubescent angst over the origin and meaning of life was submerged under another pursuit altogether—music. Equipped with my cousin's flute, I started lessons and was good at it. My family had several talented musicians, and my band director said I had talent for the flute. I formulated a new escape plan: if I would practice enough and keep my grades high, I could get a scholarship to college, move away, and never come back. The plan seemed realistically achievable, so I practiced diligently. Practicing made it possible for me to be alone much of the time, and playing music allowed me to express emotions for which I had no words.

It would almost be accurate to say that during my teenage years music became my god. Most of my time, energy, and attention went toward practicing to become the best flute player I could possibly be. All other normal teenage pursuits, such as a social life, were sacrificed to music and my plan of escape. However, it's probably more accurate to say that I was my own god. Completely self-focused, my constant concern was how well I played, how I looked on stage, and how I would measure up against other players at auditions and competitions. I lived for the praise of my teacher and thought I was superior to others because

Chapter Two

of my talent. In this shallow, meaningless existence, thoughts of suicide were frequent.

By the beginning of my senior year of high school, I had attained an advanced level of competence on the flute. The goal of my plan was in sight. With just one more year of intense effort, I would be free. But I was soon to learn just how fragile my own plans were.

One gloomy, drizzly Wednesday evening in October of my senior year, as I was driving home from church choir practice, the driver of a truck ran a red light just at the moment I crossed the intersection. The truck smashed me into a block wall, and I was trapped inside the car—which had been crunched into half its normal length—for quite some time, unconscious and not breathing. Later I learned that, until a small-built policeman came to the scene, nobody could squeeze in to rescue me. He managed to pull my bloody body from the car. It was already blue from lack of oxygen. Police laid my body out on the street and covered it as dead.

They called a local funeral director to the scene to retrieve my body. As he later told my parents, although the police had covered me up as dead, he refused to give me up for dead. Ignoring the fact that I'd been without oxygen for so long, he attempted to resuscitate me. Eventually I began to breathe. At the emergency room, the doctors told my parents that if I ever woke up, I would be a "vegetable." Many hours later, I woke up in the intensive care unit, my head bruised and swollen, with a severe concussion, and with my fingers still blue—but arguing my point that it was not I who had run the red light.

It was a miracle that I was alive and still had my mental faculties. The shattered glass from the windshield had cut within millimeters of my eyes, but they were both intact. I didn't fully appreciate these facts. The left side of my mouth was so badly torn that the nerves were severed completely, leaving it numb and uncontrollable as far as playing the flute was concerned. And, of course, this became my only concern. There were only

The Heart-Changer

three months to go before my college auditions. Everything I had hoped for was at stake.

With a great deal of work, I played the college auditions with a head still reeling from the concussion, and I did receive scholarships. But I didn't play well enough to be accepted at the conservatory of my dreams. This was a devastating disappointment to me, but a relief to my parents. They preferred that I attend a smaller conservatory at a "religious" university. Their relief was premature and unwarranted.

My years of diligent practice paid off at this small conservatory, putting me, a freshman, far ahead of the other flutists. My professor gave me positions and privileges usually reserved for upperclassmen, and I became haughtier than ever.

The fact that the university was a "religious school" was no advantage. One of the required courses for freshmen was Introduction to the Bible. The mission of the professor was to disprove the validity of the Bible and the very existence of God—and to convert every student to his own disbelief. For hours at a time, we endured his reasoning and questions: "A miracle is an event outside the possibilities of natural phenomena. Have you seen a miracle in your lifetime? Have you witnessed a blind man receive his sight? Ever been around when a deaf person was suddenly able to hear? Ever seen anyone raised from the dead? Of course not. So, if the Bible is true and God is real, why would miracles occur in Bible times but not now? The Bible is a fable. No loving God would allow people to be blind or deaf or born with birth defects. There is no God."

I never considered that the very fact I was alive, sitting in his classroom, able to see and to understand his words, was a miracle. Other than my earlier private studies in evolution, I had never encountered such questioning of the Bible and God. I'd certainly never encountered such open scorn. My weak faith, what little there was, crumbled. Some students were brave enough to argue with the professor, but it was his classroom, and he always won. Many times I left class in tears of confusion.

Chapter Two

I'd always been able to parrot back any teacher's ideas on a test to receive a good grade, and I spewed this professor's arguments to keep my honor roll standing, but it went much deeper. All the strife, the Darwinian doubt, the disappointment and depression in my life fed into his ideas. I thought perhaps the professor was right—maybe there was no God.

One afternoon in a discussion after a test, the professor gave me a smile of approval. I was finally "getting it." Later that evening, after dark, I went to the campus chapel, determined either to feel God's presence or to give up on Him. I stood alone in the dark chapel, and all I felt was fear. As I left, I said to myself, "Well, I guess I'm on my own now."

On My Own

With this formal rejection of God, my life took on a new dimension of torment and hellishness. As I officially turned my back on Him, I embraced the lie that freedom meant doing whatever seemed good to me.

I became outwardly rebellious and immoral. For the first time, I acted out on a suicidal urge. My self-pity led to many excuses to drown my sorrows in alcohol. My attitude became more and more disrespectful toward the faculty. I stopped practicing the flute as often and as intensely. At my final flute jury, in which I played for the entire woodwind faculty, they praised me for doing even better than before. I told them they had no idea what they were talking about and swore I would never return.

My lifestyle bore no resemblance to my earlier years. I had grown up in a rural area. In high school, I had dated only two or three times, and had kissed only a little. Now I was on my own in a large city, deeply involved in my very first romantic relationship. Our "love" was mostly a combination of drunkenness, mutual rebellion against authority, and lust. Our carelessness resulted in an unplanned and certainly unwanted pregnancy. When I told my boyfriend, his first response was, "Did you make an appointment

The Heart-*Changer*

to get it taken care of?" He meant an abortion, of course. He feared his life plans would be interrupted.

My fears were entirely different. Oh, yes, I was embarrassed, and my pride was hurt because I had "made a mistake." But far deeper and stronger than that, I knew what was within me—the bitterness and depression I could barely contain from moment to moment. My childhood had been spent regretting my very existence. As I tried to imagine myself as a parent, I could only see myself unleashing all of that hopeless bitterness on an innocent child. This was my biggest fear. And in my mind, the mind of one who had contemplated suicide so many times, there was no value to life. I made the appointment.

The night before the appointment, I had a vivid dream about the child—my son. He had dark hair and eyes like his father. In my dream, he was about two years old, happily playing and singing. I told my boyfriend about the dream and how realistic it was, that perhaps it was a warning not to go through with the abortion. He wasn't persuaded. I was too frightened and too focused on myself to heed the warning.

At the clinic, I took comfort in the information the counselor told me—that the fetus which was going to be removed from my body was just a blob of tissue bearing no resemblance to a human being at all. My mind went back to illustrations I'd seen in my biology textbook, showing how humans undergo something of a process of evolution in the womb—from looking like an indistinguishable blob, to resembling a fish, then an animal, until a more human appearance formed late in the pregnancy. (In my studies, I had failed to realize that those old illustrations weren't accurate.) I wanted to believe it—just a blob of tissue. Deep inside, I knew better, and I hated myself. I hated the doctor. I hated my boyfriend. I just hated.

What happened that day—the murder of my own son—left scars so profound that I buried them very deeply within. I broke up with the child's father within months, and nobody else knew what I'd done. I told absolutely no one. I coped just as I did with everything else. I kept quiet and went on as if nothing at all had happened, refusing to feel the pain.

I kept my word and did not return to classes at the small conservatory, but instead worked at a music store and commuted hundreds of miles each week for lessons with the principal flautist of the symphony orchestra in the city where I had wanted to attend conservatory for years.

Meanwhile, it had become obvious that one of the consequences of the car accident was going to be daily severe migraine headaches. Sometimes they were so blindingly painful that I thought I couldn't endure. Another consequence was that my eyesight was affected in a way no doctor seemed to be able to correct. I was seeing double. Even with one eye shut, I saw two images. Reading music became extremely difficult.

I auditioned again at the desired conservatory, playing all the music from memory, and was accepted. But by the time I was able to attend this conservatory of my dreams, I could no longer read music well enough to compete. In my flute lessons my teacher frequently asked me to sight-read. I saw not only the real notes, but also double images either above or below the real ones. It was so confusing that I couldn't play, but I didn't know how to explain it to my teacher. He accused me of being drunk or on drugs. After several months of this, I couldn't go on. Music could no longer be my life. My sense of identity collapsed.

The double vision was from irreversible damage in a specific area of my brain from the car accident. Deep inside I resented God and life itself—but all this was very, very deep inside. On the surface, I was just numb. I used the same coping mechanism that had kept me alive and functioning since childhood: I didn't feel anything and just kept going. So, with barely a whimper and no explanation whatsoever to my parents, I changed my major and began the study of music from other cultures. I had to transfer out of the conservatory to the anthropology department.

At first, I thought studying anthropology would be a good change. I had a faint intellectual fascination with other cultures.

Beyond that, I thought perhaps I could find some universal truth that would help me understand why people went on living. But even this pursuit turned out to be pointless. Eventually I realized that most of the conclusions prominent anthropologists had reached had been based on information that was, at best, incomplete and, at worst, false. I continued in anthropology simply to graduate, but my dim interest in it could not distract me from the depression that grew far worse during this time.

In fact, my lifelong depression deepened to a life-threatening state. I began to cut myself, usually on the arms and wrists, to externalize the intense emotional pain within, even if the relief was only momentary. I was barely hanging on. My identity as a musician was gone. No longer part of the social circle in the conservatory, I became all but anonymous in the larger university campus. In each anthropology class I became more and more steeped in atheistic evolutionary theory and finally reached a point where I fully accepted the proposition that all life was just a meaningless mistake. I felt it was futile even to resent God, and I began to think of Him merely as a figment of humanity's collective imagination. Life had absolutely no meaning at all. Going from class to class, I could barely contain the emotional pain boiling within me, and thoughts of suicide were constantly in my mind. I repeatedly heard a voice say, "Who do you love?" and I realized I loved no one. I was walking death, emotionally and spiritually. I tried various hedonistic diversions and perversions to escape, but these left me feeling even emptier.

In spite of all this, I graduated with honors. The way I'd learned to handle problems from an early age—to bury them and stay busy trying to be the best at whatever I did—paid off outwardly, even if inwardly I was completely bound up with hopelessness.

I had no real desire to be a lawyer, but a strong need to be independent and self-supporting, so I went on to law school—which was not exactly a fitting prescription to ease my depression. Law school was like reliving the strife and arguing I'd longed to escape as a child. I hated it with every fiber of my being from the first moment of the first class. But, as usual, I buried all that and worked as hard as I could.

During the summer after my first year of law school, I went on a short spiritual search, inspired by the national attention given to a movie about Ghandi. His biography told of his fascination with Jesus' Sermon on the Mount, and this stirred something inside me. For about a month, I sat on my apartment floor reading chapters five through seven in the book of Matthew, comparing Jesus' words to the teaching of the *Bhagavad Gita*, which I'd acquired after reading Ghandi's biography. I hungered for truth, and my heart longed for peace, but both seemed so distant and unattainable. I could read and understand the words on the surface, but the deeper meaning eluded me. Resigned to my bitter fate, I put my attention back on law school.

My first year grades had earned me a spot on the law review staff. When I received this news mid-way through the summer, I tried to be happy about my accomplishment, but it meant nothing to me. I just felt emptiness. Since childhood, I'd suspected that there could be some meaning to life in giving and receiving love, but from my experiences I had concluded that this was not an option for me. Instead, I'd kept going on the thought that I could possibly create happiness for myself by achieving a high a level in some field. But my attainment in music had been stripped away from me, and my academic achievements in law school left me feeling as empty as a gaping canyon. In my analysis, the pain of life far outweighed any pleasure. Therefore, there was no point in it at all. So, before the second year of law school began, I told my closest friend that unless I found something to live for by Christmas, I would "pull my own plug," meaning I would commit suicide. Enough was enough.

Reason for Living

One late September afternoon in my second year, I was working at the law school information desk when a classmate rounded the corner with a man I'd never met. My classmate was just passing through with her friend, but she stopped by to introduce him. This was the day I met Stephen Shedroff. There were tender feelings between us even at our first meeting. We soon became inseparable. Steve became my reason for living, and on December 15, we were married. I met my deadline by ten days.

The marriage ceremony itself was an indication of where Steve and I were spiritually. He was Jewish but hadn't been raised according to Jewish observance or tradition. We were married by a municipal court judge, and the only special instruction I gave before the wedding was that he delete every reference to God from the ceremony. At one point near the end, the judge either disregarded or forgot my instruction and said something about having exchanged our vows "before God and these witnesses." At the mention of God, I scoffed out loud. Steve characterized himself as an atheist, and I was willing to be tagged with that label as well.

With Steve I let down my guard to feel a little emotion, and our first year of marriage was good. We were both content and enjoyed each other's company. I cut to a part-time schedule at law school, and Steve worked only as much as his health would permit. He had been diabetic since age seven, and sometimes he had serious physical struggles. Near the end of our first year of marriage, his trips to the emergency room became more and more frequent. Even with repeated emergency hospitalizations, Steve never took his doctors' admonitions seriously, and we began arguing about his noncompliance. He had battled depression as well, and soon the arguments were too much for him. He left and went to stay with an attorney friend. I was completely devastated during the months of our separation. Thoughts of suicide, again,

Chapter Two

became frequent and enticing. Only the possibility that I could somehow be reunited with Steve gave me strength to resist killing myself.

Eventually I thought of a plan to get him back. He loved to spend time downtown in the city, so I found a decent apartment we could afford there, right in the middle of all the places he liked to go. We had a few more months of happiness, but location alone could not hold things together for long. It was my last year of law school, and we began arguing about my decision not to practice law upon graduation. Steve had the idea that he'd be happier in New York. I manipulated the situation by making him believe that I wanted to remain in Ohio, even though it wasn't true at all. Using negotiation skills I'd learned in law school against my own husband, I made an offer to Steve that I'd move to New York with him on the condition that I wouldn't have to be an attorney. He agreed.

On a cold January day, Steve left for a short trip to New York with his photography portfolio. Our plan was that he would get a job as a photographer, as he was quite talented, so that everything would be all set when I graduated in May. When he arrived in New York, he called to ask that I send a copyright stamp he had forgotten, and he asked me to pack it in a small box which I'd find in his top dresser drawer. When I opened the box to put in the copyright stamp, I found his wedding ring. My heart broke—no, shattered into pieces. I called him immediately only to find that he was at a very boisterous party. We couldn't hear each other over the music and loud voices, including women's voices. I was stunned and crushed by the rejection. It was as if I had finally split open inwardly to give way to the seething, oozing anger and bitterness that had always been beneath the surface in my heart, just as the crust of the earth splits from the pressure of flowing lava beneath it. All my life I had buried the anguish of being unwanted deep inside, and now its eruption threatened me to the core.

The Heart-*Changer*

Drawing on the only thing I had—my defense mechanisms dating back from early childhood—I decided I would hurt no more. My heart closed up, and I went numb. I vowed that I would not let Steve or anyone else hurt me ever again, and I began making decisions from a steely cold perspective. By coincidence, within a day or so, I found that in prior weeks I had failed to record a $500 deposit to my checking account. With this windfall, I had enough to file for a divorce. And I moved out.

Even though Steve returned from New York, I saw him only twice ever again. The first time, I ran into him on the street and nagged him about the expenses he'd charged on my credit card in New York. The second time was on a Saturday evening in early April after I'd spent a day researching at the law school library. At dusk I got on a bus to go back downtown, and I didn't see Steve until after the bus had already started moving. He stood in the street about a half a block up, apparently having seen me board the bus. I'll never forget watching the headlights of the bus reflect in his glasses, wondering if he'd move out of the way.

Later in April, I had the same dream three times. It began at the bottom of a grave, seen from the perspective of the one in it, as if a movie camera moved up the wall of the grave and out, so that I could see grass, and then feet, then legs, then the entire gathering of people. I was there in the group. Then the one who viewed us all standing there, the one from whose perspective I was seeing this dream, went up and beyond the gathering and left altogether. Even the first time I had this dream, I awoke knowing it meant Steve was going to die, but in my self-centeredness, it never occurred to me that I should actually do something to reach out to him. After the third time, I told my mother, "I don't think this divorce will ever go through. I think Steve will be dead before we go to court." Yet I didn't even try to call him.

On May 6, my last day of law school, I was getting ready to leave my early morning job as a baker in a local restaurant at 7:00 a.m. I planned to go back to my apartment, type a final paper, turn it in and be done with law forever. The telephone

Chapter Two

rang as I was heading toward the front door of the restaurant, and I answered it on the way out. I was surprised to hear Steve's mother's voice. She was crying—wailing in a way only a Jewish mother can do. "Stephen is dead."

"WHAT?"

"Stephen is dead."

"WHAT? HOW?"

"His heart—his heart."

"NO!" I slammed the phone so hard that it broke. I ran through the kitchen to the back alley and pounded the brick wall until the pain brought me to my senses.

The little African-American man who washed dishes in the mornings came to the alley to get me. Steve's mother was on the phone again. This time I had to sit down and listen. Steve had been in the hospital due to a heart attack since April 18, barely stabilized. Suddenly in the early morning hours of May 6, he had died of another massive heart attack.

My mind raced back to the last time I had spoken with his mother. It had been only a week or so before, certainly within the time in which Steve had been in the hospital. I asked her why she hadn't told me during that conversation. She said she had called me by mistake, as Steve had given her my number when she'd asked for the number of his attorney friend. Immediately, I knew the real question was why I hadn't even asked about him. If I had simply asked, surely she would have told me he was in the hospital. From that moment forward, I felt that if I had only been with him, things would have been different.

By 4:00 p.m. on the day of Steve's death, I was on a plane with his parents and his body, going to Miami for his burial the next day. Even though Steve's family had not raised him in a traditionally Jewish manner, upon his death everything became very Jewish. He had to be buried by sundown the next day.

When we arrived in Miami, we visited both sets of grandparents, as well as Steve's brother, aunt, uncle, and cousins. Somehow, at each stop at least one person found a way to take me aside to tell me that I was to blame for Steve's death. In my heart, I couldn't have agreed more.

At the graveside funeral the next day, I felt like an outsider even though I sat in the middle of the front row. A rabbi pinned a black ribbon on my lapel, then another rabbi cut it with a razor. The symbolism cut my heart. I wept uncontrollably throughout the service, but honestly it wasn't just from grief over his death. To the others, it must have appeared that I was sobbing and gasping in mourning for Steve, but it was more than that. As I stood at Steve's grave, the reservoir of sorrow tore open within me. All the rejection, the losses, the abortion, the meaninglessness came gushing out for those few moments and left me utterly wrung out and limp. I refused to leave until there was simply not a minute to spare to get me back to the airport. As I was leaving the graveside, Steve's grandmother told me, "Now we know you loved him." I didn't have the heart to tell her the truth.

Upon returning to Ohio, I couldn't go through a normal grieving process, because if I allowed myself to feel any pain associated with Steve's death, I would have to face the belief that I was responsible for it. The guilt was too overwhelming. But even though I tried to feel nothing, my emotions refused to stay completely buried. They manifested in more profound depression, suicide attempts, bitterness, and hostility.

I did have to face the issue of whether there is life after death. As it turned out, my commitment to atheism was weak. I knew there was a God. In fact, when Steve and I were still together I'd visited the religion section of the bookstore where he worked and read a book about Jesus while waiting for his shift to end. He asked what in the world I was doing, and the event prompted a conversation about the beliefs each of us held growing up. Now that Steve was gone, I was facing the logical end of what I had believed, or at least heard: Steve was in hell because of his rejection of God and of Jesus. This anguish was much, much more than I could handle.

Chapter Two

I began to attend Catholic masses for the first time in my life with a friend from law school and was impressed by the prayers for the dead, which seemed to imply there was something I could do to help Steve. I moved back to my hometown where nobody knew I'd been married at all, and it became even more important to me to honor Steve's memory. I decided to convert to Catholicism so that I could pray and do penance for him. I wanted to better his condition in any way possible.

As part of the conversion process, I met with a priest weekly for instruction. I admit I understood very little. I remember talking to the priest about the time between my first and second year of law school when I'd read the Sermon on the Mount. I recall asking the priest, "What's the big deal about Jesus' death anyway? So many people talk about His death, but shouldn't we really be concentrating on how He lived?" Even though I didn't have a clue why Jesus died, I officially became a Catholic at the Easter vigil on April 18—exactly one year after Steve's first heart attack.

In the weeks leading up to my conversion to Catholicism, I must have prayed hundreds of rosaries and dozens of novenas. I read the daily devotionals and attended mass at least one time each day. I maintained an extremely cheerful appearance, but there was no change inwardly. And there was certainly no change after my "conversion."

Sleep evaded me, especially after an event that happened on the eve of the anniversary of Steve's death. In the middle of the night I was awakened by an ugly, otherworldly creature dancing before my eyes. The features of this being's face swirled and morphed into progressively more frightening forms. It kept repeating, "Ha, ha, ha! He's in hell, and there's nothing you can do about it!" After mass the next day, the priest anointed my palms with oil, supposedly as some protection. This demonic creature appeared to me only once, but other dreams were filled with life-like encounters with Steve in my apartment. I was afraid to sleep.

The Heart-*Changer*

I remained a Catholic only a few months. At my "conversion," I was as sincere as I was capable of being, but my motivation was primarily the swelling panic over Steve's fate. Afterwards, I was frightened by the experience with the demonic creature, but strangely I chose to ignore its taunt that there was nothing I could do to help Steve. I decided to become a nun so I could devote my whole life to doing penance for Steve. This decision caught the attention of a prominent Catholic man. He started popping up unexpectedly and uninvited at places I frequented, including my apartment building. Our discussions usually centered on his personal problems, but, actually, this was a comfort to me. Focusing on his problems made it easier to avoid dealing with my own. A friendship developed, and gradually it went beyond appropriate boundaries as we spent more time together. I could have stopped these encroachments on my space and my body, but I didn't. He became dependent on me, and I took comfort in the fact that at least somebody wanted me. Also, I felt safer from demonic visitations when I wasn't alone. This illicit relationship was eventually exposed, and I experienced a great deal of condemnation and rejection from the Catholic community. But it was just another pound on a very heavy load I had carried for so long that, after a short while, it didn't make much difference. I went on, as usual.

In the next years, I punished myself by cutting off relationships with people who seemed to love me and instead pursued only abusive, destructive relationships. I sought counseling, and even went to a psychiatrist, but it didn't help. Two doctors freely prescribed pain pills for migraine headaches and endometriosis, and the narcotics kept me in a welcome state of numbness. Instead of dealing with my own issues, I made the conscious decision to solve others' problems, even though they inevitably made mine worse. This unwise strategy led to my second marriage, an ill-fated relationship that lasted just a little over a year.

All this was happening contemporaneously with my first years of law practice. I hated my job almost as much as I had hated law school. Eventually I wound up out of work, completely broke, and living in my mother's apartment.

My health had weakened to a serious state. Even so, I underwent surgery to relieve the endometriosis and afterward realized I was addicted to narcotics. I cut myself off and went through terrible withdraw symptoms and intense physical pain. As hard as I tried to suppress my emotional pain, profound anguish was my constant companion. I was lost in utter hopelessness. There seemed to be no end to life's disappointments, and my lack of love had been proven over and over. I was sick in body, mind, soul, and spirit—desperately sick.

Divine Preservation

My depression was so deep that I decided I would, indeed, commit suicide by a radical and foolproof, if somewhat messy, method. Just as I headed up the stairs to the bathtub with a set of sharp knives in hand, the doorbell rang. I was in no mood to see anyone, and I certainly didn't want to be interrupted, but for some reason I threw the knives on the landing and answered the door. There stood a woman holding a box of small plaques. She handed me a card which read, "Good day! I am deaf. I make my living by selling these plaques. Please find one you like and pay me what you feel it is worth." Her smile was like a tiny ray of light to me. To be polite, I looked through her collection and was thinking I had no use for the butterflies, puppies, and kittens on these plaques. Then I saw one of a different kind. It depicted a sculpture of a small child leaning into a large hand, with this text: "I WILL NOT FORGET YOU. I HAVE HELD YOU IN THE PALM OF MY HAND. ISAIAH 49:15." These words instantly penetrated my heart in a powerful way. In tears, I gave the woman my last five dollars and held onto the plaque, literally for dear life. For just a moment, the hope that there was a God who cared about me was enough.

A month or so later, I borrowed money to visit an old friend from law school days who had moved to San Diego. She knew I was depressed and felt I needed a change, even a temporary one. I was afflicted with a bad cold during the plane trip. My friend and her husband did all they could to cheer me up, including taking me to meet other friends at a mountain resort. The scenery was stunningly beautiful, but because of my illness I wasn't able to go hiking with the others. Instead, I spent time alone on the deck of the cabin under the towering pine trees. For the first time in ages, I felt peace as I rested there alone. Suddenly, I became aware of the presence of God. It was as if the whole area became holy. My mind was immediately filled with a song of praise, although it was different than any song I'd ever known or heard. It had several verses, each telling that God's hand had been on my life from the very beginning, that He would watch over me to the end, and that I could trust Him even though the end was not in sight.

I never told anyone about how God reached out to me on these two occasions. Neither did I take it upon myself to seek Him by reading the Bible, praying, or opening my heart to Him in any way. Quite the contrary, as real as these experiences had been, I still did not believe God loved me. How could He love *me*?

The memory of Steve's funeral, the only Jewish service I had ever attended, led me to go to the local synagogue, where I was warmly welcomed. Eventually, I traveled on a regular basis to a "Conservadox" synagogue two hours away, and I did my best to keep kosher for almost a year. Hearing the scriptures sung in Hebrew at the synagogue brought a deep longing for peace, but I had no idea how to get it. Looking back on my life, I saw how I had vacillated between periods of wondering, "What must I do to please God, to get Him to love me?" and periods characterized by my attitude of, "I give up! It's no use! I'll just do whatever I feel like doing, whether it's right or not!" Either way, there was no peace.

As much as I liked going to the synagogue, it reminded me that I didn't really fit in anywhere. No matter how hard I tried, I would never be a Jew. I felt I had already tried Christianity, and it didn't work. I wanted to find something that was universally true for all people for all time. What is truth, and where could I find it? It, too, seemed out of my reach.

I settled for what I knew best, which was wallowing in despair and comforting myself with self-pity. Despite how God had reached out to me, I maintained a level of depression that kept me just above the suicide level. My headaches grew worse and worse. I managed to practice law again, but I hated all the arguing and power games. My life was one disastrous relationship after another. I was angry, bitter, unforgiving, tense, and fearful.

My health conditions led me to try some experimental medicines that affected my body in a very bad way. It's no wonder that by 1992 I was diagnosed with chronic fatigue-immune dysfunction syndrome. My doctor told me in April of that year that unless I confined myself to bed rest immediately and for the foreseeable future, my illness would be lifelong and debilitating.

Nevertheless, I tried to keep working on a part-time basis because I didn't know how I'd support myself. But eventually all my body's systems started shutting down. My mother had remarried, and my kind stepfather saw to it that I could go to a clinic in Massachusetts for treatment, where one of the doctors taught me how to "follow my breath" in meditation. This simple form of meditation was the gateway to that which I eventually, and wrongfully, considered to be the best thing that ever happened to me—experiencing the bliss in meditation, which all began on that decisive morning in April 1994.

My Decisive Morning

All my life God had shown me mercy and kindness, but self-pity had kept me from realizing it. He had spared me from death and disabling injury. He had warned me of the consequences of bad decisions and had given me special awareness of His presence—in spite of the way I had despised and rejected Him, and even scoffed at Him. On that decisive morning in April 1994, when God brought Jesus and forgiveness to my mind, He reached out to me yet another time, extending His goodness toward me. But that morning I made the conscious decision to reject the Jesus of the Bible. I denied Him and chose to meditate instead.

Then the guru entered my life through those blissful experiences, and suddenly it seemed that many things in my life made sense. A lifetime of believing lies had prepared me for the guru's teachings. For example, the guru taught that mankind was a result of both God's use of evolution and a special act of creation. This resonated with my childhood struggle with Darwinism. The guru taught that all religions lead to God. This teaching that no religion was better than any other was consistent with the anti-ethnocentric view I had learned in college anthropology courses. The guru's teaching also seemed to give answers to my personal conflict and pain. When I attended the convocation in the summer of 1995, a monk answered a question from the audience about abortion: "What are the spiritual consequences of abortion for the mother and the aborted child?" The monk matter-of-factly stated that the consequences were not dire at all. The child simply returns to God to await another incarnation, he said. The mother may have to undergo an incarnation in which she is aborted, but she will just go back to God to wait also. Essentially, there was "no harm, no foul." The concept of karma and reincarnation not only made sense of all the bad things that had happened to me, but it also allowed me an intellectual escape from the guilt of the terrible things I had done. The guru taught there is no such thing as sin. If there is no sin, there is no guilt. It was I and only I who would have to pay for all those bad things, but not forever in hell. I would merely have to reincarnate on this earth to work off the bad karma I had created, until I myself would be God-realized, absorbed into God-consciousness, according to the guru. And, to my great relief, the same would be true for Steve, a very comforting thought.

I considered the guru's teachings to be the answer to all my questions about Christianity. A friend had recommended Dietrich Bonhoeffer's book, *The Cost of Discipleship*, and it helped me identify what had made me so dissatisfied with the Christianity I had observed growing up. Bonhoeffer complained of Christians who readily accept God's forgiveness but fail to accept His call to discipleship—the call to follow Jesus Christ closely. I had never seen any person live as if he or she was totally committed to Christ. And I had always wondered what I had to *do* to earn God's love. So, I was delighted with the guru's teachings that required total commitment to his path. I equated this call for total commitment with truth.

My greatest delight was the guru's teaching that my blissful experiences indicated that I was very spiritually advanced. My pride enabled me to overlook completely the real harm I had done to other people, even my own child. The guru's teachings gave me the mental framework to begin seeing myself as deserving of all the good things that were now happening to me, as I thought I must have earned them. I saw the misery of my earlier life as my own payment for past wrongs done—although I still harbored much self-pity and resentment for the emotional pain I had endured. In short, under the guru's teachings, I came to believe I had come from God and would return to God, as God. In reality I was my own god. I was my own judge, pronouncing my own sentence. Being self-focused, I fancied a light sentence for myself, and the guru's teachings seemed to give me a basis.

There is a way that seems right to man, but it leads to death. I was willing to believe lie after lie, which led to my decision to enter the ashram.

Seeking Acceptance

While attending the worldwide convocation of the guru's devotees in Los Angeles in 1995, I met several nuns and saw many more. Their smiles were ever-present. "How wonderful

The Heart-Changer

their lives must be," I thought. I wanted to be accepted to the ashram more than anything.

Part of the application process was to submit a short autobiography. I don't know how other applicants interpreted "short," but mine was about thirty-five pages long and mainly told of the change from the deep unhappiness I had endured for thirty-six years before the guru entered my life to the bliss I had experienced when he did.

The nuns on the entrance committee had read my autobiography and entire application. By the end of convocation, all things looked very hopeful for my acceptance. At last, there was promise that my life had value and purpose. I had finally found something that seemed to fill the void I'd always felt and made up for all the losses I'd experienced. For the first time, I felt loved, and the guru's teachings said that my achievements in his eyes earned me that love. According to the guru, God would reveal Himself to me if I gave Him all my effort. God alone mattered, or so I thought. I was so well-practiced at believing lies that I was unable to detect a counterfeit.

Chapter Three

~ ~ ~

Unconditional Loyalty and Devotion

The day finally came around mid-November 1995. I received the letter of final acceptance to the guru's ashram, telling me to plan to come in late January 1996. My excitement was dampened a bit with the realization that it was time to tell my family and my boss I was leaving—a difficult task, especially since I'd been so quiet about my involvement with this unfamiliar religion for the preceding eighteen months. My boss kindly agreed to allow me to work until a week or so before leaving for Los Angeles. My mother was very upset at first. Then, after a couple of weeks, my younger sister was reconciled with her after six years of their not speaking to one another. I was sure this miraculous reconciliation was brought about by the guru so that I could go.

As the reality of my upcoming departure gradually dawned on me, I had a flood of doubts. I quieted them by thinking of the seemingly miraculous events since 1994 and the way everything was coming together to make it possible for me to leave. A day before my departure, I was afflicted with a high fever. Somehow I managed to keep packing and preparing, and on January 26, 1996, I left. I traveled two thousand miles for the purpose of devoting my life to the truth—as I thought it to be.

I arrived at dusk to the welcome of a dozen or so nuns along with the housemother of the postulant ashram, or "PA," as I would thereafter call my new home. It was a roomy house surrounded by a good-sized yard with mature trees, enclosed by a six-foot high steel-barred fence. The PA was across the street

The Heart-*Changer*

from the "mother center," a gated estate consisting of several spacious buildings situated amidst lush trees and gardens. The gate was locked behind me, and I officially renounced the world as a monastic disciple.

I signed a "resident disciple pledge," which was actually a series of pledges to the guru and his organization. The first was "my unconditional loyalty and devotion to God, Jesus Christ, Bhagavan Krishna; and to the Gurus of this path." I further pledged to "be steadfast in my communion with God through daily meditation," and "to reflect His joy, His love, and His peace in my every word, thought, and action." The various clauses of the pledge included promises to obey with devotion all the rules of ashram life; to refrain from gossip, negative or critical talk; to avoid arguments and displays of temper or anger; to follow strictly the rule of celibacy, obedience, loyalty, and simplicity; to refrain from mixing with members of the opposite sex; and to refrain from engaging in any kind of sexual practices. I had no hesitation in signing this document. I actually believed I could reflect God's love, joy, and peace in everything I did and said.

At the first meeting with a senior nun in the personnel department, I reviewed some of the practical aspects of my new life. As part of our training, the monastic disciples performed the labor necessary to keep the ashram and organization running, in exchange for our room and board and the sum of $30.00 per month. Postulants, the newcomers, were responsible for paying for their own health care expenses and supplying their own clothing. We wore dresses, jumpers, or skirts, with hemlines hitting mid-calf or below.

I was eager to fulfill all my pledges and assumed I had the ability to comply based on the willpower I had developed earlier in life. I had no concern for my material needs, though I took virtually no savings at all.

I was one of two new American postulants to arrive that day to a house full of women from Germany, Canada, Japan, China, England, and the Philippines. In our honor, that evening one of

Chapter Three

our German housemates cooked an unusual spaghetti dinner, and we ate Indian-style, sitting on the living room floor. It was one of very few meals that would not be eaten in total silence. That night, there was much giggling as we chatted and ate the strange spaghetti concoction. It seemed to contain every spice in the cupboard, and I later learned there were bananas in it as well! Vegetarian cooking was never so imaginative.

The mood was lighthearted as our housemother guided the discussion after dinner. We sat in a circle, and she asked us to tell the story of how we had come to the guru and his teachings. According to tradition, because I had been the last to arrive, I would be the first to tell my story.

Never having been a member of a meditation group, or having spent any length of time around other devotees, I had no idea that I might be breaching some unwritten rule of etiquette or decorum when I launched into my story, beginning with the day of the chela incident, and including the bliss I had experienced in meditation during the weeks just prior to finding the guru. I simply told my story, unaware that it was in the least unusual. With an uplifted tone of voice, I finished my story, joyous from reliving the events of 1994. Expecting to hear more of the same, I was surprised to hear most of the others tell about how a friend or relative had told them of the guru's books or invited them to a meeting. All of the postulants listened intently to the others' stories, and we were happy for one another no matter what had brought us to the guru. But I detected disapproval from my housemother for the way I had spoken, and the coming months would reveal that my hunch was right.

Although I meant nothing by it, apparently telling my story was not the right thing to do. It certainly started things off on the wrong foot with my housemother. In later conversations, it became abundantly clear that she perceived my story as flagrant boasting. She explained that there were monastic disciples, including her, who had been in the ashram for decades and had never had the slightest of any such experiences—hearing the cosmic vibration ("om"), seeing the "spiritual eye," or experiencing bliss in kriya yoga meditation. Therefore, my housemother instructed that my experiences were to be considered as candy to a baby. I should no longer take such delight in them, but rather be willing to tell God and guru that I didn't need these experiences anymore. If I could continue without such candy, then my commitment and loyalty would be proven.

I was confused. I had relied on the lessons and books, which taught that my experiences were actually the goals of meditation and were indicators of spiritual advancement. Now I was told to put them aside. And the person instructing me to do so was the guru's "channel," or spokesperson to me—as this is how we were taught to view and understand our assigned counselor. Anything my housemother said to me, I had to consider as coming directly from the guru himself.

I was determined to plow through any confusion or difficulty. After all, I was relying on "the only savior of mankind"—my own "progressive dynamic will." My determination and willpower would be my salvation, according to the guru. In my estimation, I had enough willpower for three people, so I was quite confident that I could not fail to achieve my salvation.

Although my *faux pas* at the first dinner in the PA was truly innocent, my housemother's impression of me as prideful was certainly not baseless. For one thing, all the old bitterness and resentment was still very much in my heart. None of the blissful meditative experiences had eradicated the nasty poison of strife and contention which could bubble up instantly upon sufficient provocation. The energy it took to keep this nastiness suppressed usually appeared to others as arrogance, or at least extreme self-confidence. It was part of me that I'd always hated, yet was unable to change. But I had quite a bit of genuine arrogance in me as well. My pride entered the ashram with me, and I was ever ready to act on my belief that, if given the opportunity to prove my point about an issue, I could persuade any reasonable person to agree with me out of sheer logic. Living in submission to authority under rules I was expected to follow unquestioningly would be quite an adjustment.

There were many other adjustments to monastic life. Postulants were to become experts at housecleaning and gardening. We spent hours each day learning and doing both, not simply for their own sake but also as a demonstration of spiritual commitment. For instance, if my cleaning area was dusty, or my gardening area had weeds, it was a sign that something was wrong in my spiritual life. There were endless discussions on such topics each week in meetings and classes.

Our daily routine began at about 5:00 a.m. for at least a half hour of individual meditation. We then dressed and performed brief morning duties before group meditation, which lasted forty-five minutes. After eating breakfast in silence, we studied the guru's teachings silently for an hour. Next, we dispersed for an hour of gardening, followed by an hour of housekeeping. Noon meditation lasted thirty minutes. Lunch in silence was next, and then we were quickly off to afternoon duties. All of this was punctuated by extremely quick changes of clothing, as we were allowed certain places in certain clothes, but not others. About 4:00 p.m., we practiced hatha yoga, or body positions. After one more quick change of clothes, we went to group meditation with the senior nuns, followed by light recreation and dinner in silence. Each evening we had classes, counseling meetings, or group meditations. This routine was the basic schedule, but there were constant variations.

Each nun was accountable to a superior nun, who acted as her spiritual counselor, and each was responsible to complete her own "introspection chart," as it was called, which the counselor reviewed monthly. Every day we recorded on the chart how long we meditated, whether we participated in each activity, and, most importantly, what our mood or attitude was like throughout the day. This was the supreme question. Bad moods, bad attitudes, and negative thoughts could not and would not be tolerated. But, oh, how they arose! It would be an understatement to say that there was spiritual and other competition between postulants. In such an environment, differences and bad moods were sure to spring up, so this was often the topic of group counseling meetings in the PA.

All of us postulants, however, were eagerly trying to change and improve ourselves. All of us were finding our own way of adjusting, honoring our pledge to the guru, and learning our new roles in life. Life in the ashram was not easy. But we were reminded quite often that life in the world would be even more difficult.

The Guru and Grace

For new postulants, morning study sessions were devoted to listening to recorded lectures by one of the highest senior nuns who had been in the ashram during the guru's lifetime. She spoke as his representative to instruct us about his expectations, often using her own personal experiences with him as examples. The lectures covered the written and unwritten rules of the ashram as well as the "spiritual principles" behind them.

Each day I took copious notes. The lecturer taught that if we followed not only the letter of the rules, but also the spirit or principle behind them, we would actually be following the guru himself, and this would "lead to our salvation." We were assured that if we did so, we would not fail to attain our goal, which was self-realization, also called God-realization—to be like God; or, actually, to be God, merged with His bliss. On the other hand, if we failed at any of the rules or spiritual principles, we would be lacking in a quality that would keep us from our goal.

First and foremost, we were to keep our initial enthusiasm. From my notes, a close paraphrase of this lecture would be: "What you think and do, how you act, whether with enthusiasm and joy, or with the lack thereof—these God watches. You are either building merit to gain blessings or not, depending on your own effort. Therefore, you must put forth one hundred percent effort at all times, doing things with willingness and cheerfulness. Otherwise, instead of progressing, you will accrue bad karma, and God will not accept the offering of your service. Even if you just do little things for God, if you do them cheerfully, He will consider your little offerings and you will get His attention."

An important lecture on a following day was about grace. We learned that if we gave God all of our effort, then, when He willed it, in His time, He would give us grace, through the guru. The senior nun described grace in this way: "Imagine pushing a canoe out into the water from the shore. It is hard at first, and takes much effort while the canoe is hung up on the sand or mud. But when the bottom of the canoe is finally free, and it glides in the water, going forward takes little effort. This is what grace is like. You have to put forth much effort constantly, just as it would be necessary to push the canoe out from the shore. When God, through the guru, contributes grace, it will be as if you begin to meet no resistance for a little while. You can compare it to the hypothetical canoe when it is finally afloat. With one hundred percent of your effort and God's contribution of grace, through the guru, you will occasionally find yourselves gliding along with little trouble."

I was biblically ignorant, so it never occurred to me that this description of grace was completely contrary to the Bible's definition: grace is a gift of God, altogether unearned and unmerited, which He gives freely and eagerly! I didn't even stop to reason that grace and works are mutually exclusive. And I had no idea that God offered total forgiveness by grace, so that my salvation was not dependent on my own efforts. I didn't know that God was ready and willing to pour out His grace to change me and empower me to live according to His ways, and I surely didn't grasp what Jesus had really done for me. No, I was a new postulant, trying very hard to fit in and live up to my pledge of unconditional loyalty and devotion to the guru. There was no time for critical thinking. The busy postulant schedule was not conducive to pondering deeply the steady stream of teaching I was receiving. I was just trying to absorb and apply bits of it as I could. I just accepted the taped lecture's teaching and moved on.

The guru's teachings contained many different principles that seemed rather disjointed and even incongruous, so I chose one central, overarching theme by which to live. The principle that felt right to me was that "the only savior of mankind is a constantly progressive dynamic will." I would "will" myself to salvation, by willing to do the right things as the guru taught. I would practice kriya yoga meditation as perfectly and as often as possible, and I would be the best monastic disciple I could possibly be. If I got a little grace now and then, all the better.

The guru taught that if we monastic disciples were faithful to the end, at our death he would take a larger portion of our bad karma to further us in our next incarnation. Again, I never stopped to think about the logical inconsistency between the teaching that my own dynamic will would save me, and the concept that, in the end, grace would also be necessary. In retrospect, it is remarkable to me that all of us under the guru's teachings recognized that we would have to have grace. But of course, the grace we were hoping for would come at the price of our hard work. Whether we recognized it or not, or whether we even thought about it, on some level we realized the hopelessness of purifying ourselves of bad karma by our own good works and meditation. We would have to rely on the guru to take it—if we earned this privilege.

This concept of one person's taking another's bad karma seemed believable to me, again, because of certain experiences of my own. At times I had asked the guru to let me take another person's headache, sore throat, anxiety, or the like, to work out the other person's karma on my own body. Most of the time when I made these requests, the other person was immediately relieved of her own symptoms as I was immediately afflicted with them. By these experiences, I became convinced of two things. I believed it was, indeed, possible to take on another's karma. And

I believed I was approaching a high level of spiritual attainment, as the guru taught that only advanced devotees could do this.

Satan himself oppresses people with sickness, and at times he chooses to alleviate that oppression temporarily to further his purposes of deception. Only God can truly heal. Apparently it was part of Satan's plot to deceive me in this way. And yes, I was greatly deceived. But this deception would later backfire on the deceiver! Eventually I would understand that the guru's promise to take my bad karma was a lie. But that would take a while longer. I wasn't yet ready to hear God's true voice.

Little Convincing "Proofs"

At the ashram, as before, I trusted my feelings and experiences as my main source of truth, or to validate that which I thought was truth. I was not alone. Throughout my stay, there was no shortage of stories from other nuns of many experiences in which the guru had supernaturally supplied their particular desires and needs. We were taught that, if we developed a desire, the guru was obliged to satisfy it, lest that one desire create the need for an additional incarnation. Even before I went to the ashram, in my day-to-day life within the guru-disciple relationship, I'd felt that the guru was seeing to the details of my life, so I was not surprised when I heard such stories after entering.

Most of these fulfilled desires were for little things. After about a month, I developed a craving for pizza, but of course I didn't express this desire to anyone. Within a day or so, we had pizza for lunch, and the postulants received a larger portion than usual. We ate lunch in silence according to the rule, then began to clear the table. One of the German postulants broke silence with the question, "OK, who had the desire for pizza?"

"I did! But how did you know?"

"That's the way it works around here," she replied, and everyone laughed as we shared stories of the guru's generosity and supernatural provision.

One of the ways we met our desire to shop was by visiting the "VL," which was what we called the "Volunteer League Room," a storage room in which donated clothing, shoes, personal items, religious gifts, greeting cards, and various other goods were placed for the benefit of all the nuns. Very often we could go there and find exactly what we needed or wanted.

Otherwise, shopping was infrequent. We went out to a department store about every four to six weeks, and then only for about ninety minutes. Ashram rules dictated that we had to be in pairs while shopping. We would travel as a group to Pasadena or Glendale, then split up into pairs.

A particular shopping trip during my second spring at the ashram will serve as an example of how the guru, or the spirit behind him, fulfilled desires in supernatural ways.

My alarm clock had become unreliable. This was not a huge problem, as my body was accustomed to waking up at the same time every day, but I thought it best to replace the clock to be on the safe side. I told no one of my need, but I knew the kind of alarm clock I would buy. It would be a small black plastic (inexpensive) travel alarm. I had seen one on a previous shopping trip and knew exactly where to find it.

On the next trip out, I was paired with a younger postulant who needed to buy shoes. All of our time was spent on her obtaining the shoes, so that there was no time to go to a different section of the store to get the alarm clock. Instead of being concerned with my own need, for once I was patient enough to stand by and let the minutes tick away without doing any shopping of my own.

The next Monday morning, after I had completed my gardening duties at the mother center, I crossed the street to head back to my cleaning area at the PA. On this day, I happened to be alone. There in the middle of the street was a small black plastic travel alarm—exactly the one I had wanted to buy. I picked it up. It was even set to the correct time! I looked all around to see who might have dropped it, or if it had fallen from a car by accident,

Chapter Three

but no one else was around. The voice of the guru sounded in my mind, "This is for you."

Running into the PA, I broke silence to show the others. "Look at the alarm clock the guru just gave me. It's exactly like the one I wanted to buy last Saturday, but didn't have enough time!" This event was deemed so commonplace that little more than smiles and polite comments were necessary to acknowledge it.

And, indeed, as tangible as the alarm clock was, the event was not unusual. It was such "tangible proofs" that laid the groundwork for me to keep believing when the guru later spoke harsh things. These little convincing proofs kept me clinging to the guru, even when things became quite difficult.

Before entering the ashram, life with the guru had been, for the most part, happy and blissful, full of anticipation, and at times positively exciting. I thought I wanted to find God, to know Him and live my life for Him. In practical terms, this meant that I wanted to improve myself so that I could be worthy of God's love and stay in the state of bliss. It meant that, at long last, I would be loved and accepted.

After a few months, things had changed. My motives had changed. The ecstasy of infatuation had faded, and I was ever so aware that I simply wanted to undergo as few additional incarnations as possible. My focus shifted from the desire to "know God" to the desire to escape the rounds of reincarnation, simply to escape the pain of living. I learned that I had to recognize this world as delusion. I had to "die to myself" completely, eradicate bad habits, perfect the meditation techniques, and learn how to thrive in the ashram with a good attitude. All this was necessary for me to avoid living on this earth ever again, or at least as few times as possible.

The emphasis was supposed to be on "God and God alone." As devotees of the guru, we were supposed to be seeking the divine within us. Meditation was to take us to higher levels of consciousness, away from the delusive physical world and into the ethereal world of the spirit. But ashram life led me to focus on myself in new and intense ways.

Because of the requirement for formal introspection, even to the point of completing time-based introspection charts, it was impossible to go for fifteen minutes without focusing on myself—what I was thinking, how I was feeling, and what I desired. Every aspect of my life and thoughts were open to my housemother's comment on a regular basis. If I failed to express myself well, making the mistake of giving her an inaccurate impression of my thoughts or feelings, then I would have to write even more to clarify.

Beyond the introspection charts, however, ashram life for me largely degenerated to a mundane quest: eating foods that would not make me sick.

All nuns were directed to eat the meals prepared by the central kitchen, with few exceptions. Only those who had medical reasons were allowed to deviate from the main menu. Before coming, I had informed the personnel department that I must avoid wheat, eggs, and any foods containing monosodium glutamate because of severe reactions. Unbeknownst to me, the personnel office had misplaced my file, so my medical information was not available to my superiors. My housemother expected me to partake of the vegetarian meals consisting mainly of foods that made me sick, especially the meat substitute products laden with monosodium glutamate. My health steadily deteriorated, but I tried to hide it. The postulant schedule was fast and furious most of the time, and I didn't want to give the impression that I couldn't keep up.

After about eight months of eating the main menu, my health problems were mounting, so I talked to my housemother about the food issue. I explained that, because of my food sensitivities, the meals were actually like poison to me. She was displeased with my complaining and informed me that, unless I learn to eat the same food as everyone else, I very well might be asked to leave the ashram. I couldn't stand the thought of such a consequence, such a failure, so I made more of an effort to hide my symptoms.

Chapter Three

One day, when a migraine headache rendered me useless and I was confined to bed, I picked up a little New Testament (with Psalms and Proverbs) I had brought with me. I liked it because it was a children's Bible. On its cover was a drawing of Jesus with children all around Him. I found the picture comforting. The little Bible fell open to Philippians chapter three, where I read, "that I may know Him, and the power of His resurrection, and the fellowship of His sufferings, being made conformable unto His death" (Phil. 3:10 KJV). My thoughts went briefly to Jesus' sufferings. I had never understood why Jesus' death was so significant, but my suffering felt so massive at the time that I thought perhaps I might come to know God *through* it. This idea was the fuel needed to keep the flame of enthusiasm burning, the flame of my "ever-progressive, dynamic will." I determined that I would never give up.

I couldn't hide all my symptoms for long, however. By Christmas, it was difficult to breathe, and my headaches were unbearable. Because I tried to gain relief in small ways here and there without explaining why, some of my choices appeared selfish, capricious, disobedient, and even foolish to my housemother. Her impression of me was steadily declining.

As the first anniversary of entering the ashram approached, I learned that the young lady who had entered on the same day I did would soon be taking her novice vow, but I would not. Explaining the difference, my housemother at first pointed to my successes since entering, such as leading the postulant workforce during the previous summer's convocation and directing the music program at Christmas. But she said that the guru was not concerned with a devotee's hard work or talent. Even though I had put forth my best efforts and abilities, it was not enough. The guru was chiefly concerned, she said, with whether the devotee was wholly devoted to him. She felt that I was spiritually lacking in that I was not wholly devoted.

My housemother had sometimes disciplined my thinking for being too questioning and analytical. For example, early on I had read some of the archived magazines at the PA and found that the kriya instructions published during the guru's lifetime differed significantly from the instructions now given in the lessons, and I'd asked her about it. Apparently she had considered my questions to be unacceptable. Of course, there were our conversations about the food, in which she'd said I was overly critical and complaining. I had not shown that I was unconditionally loyal and devoted. I was not living up to my pledge as a postulant. My housemother was the guru's channel to me, so I had to accept her evaluation as true.

Even though I wouldn't be taking the novice vow as my companion would, we were both allowed to go on a spiritual retreat to an ashram property near Twentynine Palms, California, in January 1997. We meditated, climbed mountains, read, and enjoyed plenty of sleep. We gazed at stars and the Hale-Bopp comet. It was good to get away from the busy ashram schedule.

One of the features of the Twentynine Palms property was a small house in which the guru had written some of his most important teachings. No one could enter the house, but the porch was a shrine, and we were allowed to meditate there. I spent many hours on that porch, where the "vibrations" were supposed to be conducive to "going deep."

After a lot of reflection while on retreat, I determined that I would intensify my efforts in spiritual matters. I began meditating more seriously—two to three hours on Saturday nights and six hours each Sunday, availing myself of the quiet atmosphere in the chapels in other buildings not usually frequented by postulants. I sought to fill every spare moment with some spiritual pursuit, whether it be meditating, chanting, journaling, or reading the guru's teachings.

I did not, however, feel more devoted to the guru. Instead I felt a growing sense of restlessness because of my desire to be useful in the lives of others. The happy memories from my childhood involved our family giving anonymously to other families who had suffered misfortune, such as a house fire, even if we could

Chapter Three

give only our best hand-me-downs. As an adult, my entire legal career had centered in one way or another on providing free or reduced-fee services to low-income clients. At the ashram, I felt useless, even in my special duties.

I had been assigned to the correspondence department, at first as a secretary, but later as a beginning letter writer. I typed responsive letters to lay devotees' requests for prayer and information. However, most of the responses I typed were "canned," or pre-written, and thus seemed insincere. Worse yet, most responses to prayer requests were simply not true. My superiors instructed me to write that our letter was late because we were backlogged, but that we had been praying at the time the devotee requested it. I thought this implied we were praying specifically for each devotee's special request, and I knew we had not done that. My conscience was pricked. I began to see that even if this ostensibly "helping job" became my permanent duty, I wouldn't really be helping people. I would be nothing more than a purveyor of little white lies.

During this time of growing restlessness, the foundation laid by the "little convincing proofs," such as the pizza and alarm clock, became relevant. They became my frame of reference for evaluating things I was hearing from the guru (or the spirit behind him), things I would have otherwise found disturbing.

For example, one day in the spring of 1997, as I was returning to the PA from some meaningless duty, feeling useless and discouraged, I became aware of a commotion in a tree above the gate. A very large crow was attacking a baby songbird in its nest, as the mother bird chirped loudly in protest to no avail. I looked all around to find something, anything, to throw at the crow, but it was too late. I witnessed the crow's large beak tearing the chick apart as the mother bird impotently flapped her wings. A sick, sinking feeling overcame me, deep in my stomach. Just then, I heard these words, spoken inaudibly within, by the voice of the guru: "Let the dead bury their dead." I recognized the words as a quotation from the Bible, but at the same time I knew this was the voice of the guru telling me to give up my quest to help other people—that I needed to be concerned only with my personal walk on his path.

A few weeks later, my housemother was in isolation for health reasons, and we could communicate by letter only. She requested that I be more open with her about my feelings, so I wrote to her about the crow incident and how I interpreted it—that I had to give up my restless quest to do good in this world, as it was only delusion. My interpretation met with her wholehearted approval. I suppose it appeared that I was becoming more devoted to the guru and his path.

The little convincing proofs had worked. Or had they? My housemother's approval notwithstanding, there was still an emptiness inside me. It was emptiness the guru, his teachings, and his way of life could not fill.

Inconsistencies

The longer I stayed at the ashram, the more it became clear that something was not right. Things weren't matching up to the guru's promises. All around me, I saw nuns who had devoted themselves to the guru and monastic life for years, even decades, yet they struggled with the same personality issues as the new postulants. Were meditation and devotion really going to change me? Why would I be any different than the older, senior nuns who still had their issues, emotional problems, and personality struggles?

I began to see that changing myself was a hopeless proposition. The more I pursued humility, the supreme virtue, the less likely it was to come. Our superiors encouraged us to do little things in such a way that nobody else would know—mop floors at night after everyone else had gone to bed, or secretly clean a bathroom or someone else's cleaning area. Every time I did these things, my pride bristled at the thought of someone else getting credit. Unless I could report it on my introspection chart, how could

Chapter Three

my housemother know that I was becoming more humble? How could it demonstrate that I was living up to my pledge? But if I did some humble act, yet noticed it enough to record it on my introspection chart, didn't it really mean I had taken pride in it? Pride was already a strong enough force in my life without adding to it under the pretense of cultivating humility. Worse yet, when others did my duties as a means of gaining their own humility, I seethed with anger! There was so much about me that needed to be changed, but so little evidence that it would happen at the ashram.

Despite appearances we put on for the benefit of visitors, there seemed to be precious little genuine joy at the ashram. Each nun found her own way to cope. Some worked very long hours in their office jobs. Some modeled their lives after famous Catholic nuns. Some didn't even try to hide their self-important and callous attitudes. Others just stayed to themselves, and some rarely smiled. There were arguments over duties and rules—relatively petty disagreements that blew up out of proportion. There seemed to be only one point on which everyone seemed to agree: living in the ashram was better than living "in the world," because the world was essentially an evil place. We could always put on a show of joy or whip up a batch of enthusiasm when required, but in reality, life in the ashram was not what it appeared to be.

Another inconsistency that caught my attention was the attitude toward Christianity. The guru taught the "harmony of all religions," that all religious paths are essentially the same in that they all lead to God. Yet Christianity was the only religion ever criticized. Specifically, the guru criticized it as "churchianity" and claimed that those who merely go to church and do not practice kriya yoga cannot save themselves, let alone others. On a taped message, one of the nuns ridiculed Christians for their belief that Jesus Christ is the exclusive way to God. Even though the guru wrote that all religions lead to God, he really taught that his path was superior to any other, especially Christianity.

A picture of Jesus Christ was displayed on each altar; yet because of the emphasis on loyalty to our guru, I felt uncomfortable meditating on Jesus exclusively for any length of time. The guru's teaching made it abundantly clear that if the devotee rejects him in this lifetime, she will undergo many lifetimes before he will allow himself to be found again. For lack of loyalty in this lifetime, I would suffer the bad karma of many lifetimes of no spiritual progress, and thus many lifetimes of pain. I knew in my heart that my motive for seeking God was not pure, but rather for my own gain—in the long term, to escape more painful incarnations, and in the short term, to survive the ashram.

The guru taught that it would be beneficial to repeat mentally the phrase, "Reveal Thyself, reveal Thyself" on a constant basis, in order to coax God to give attention to us—that if we practiced this kind of mental mantra, it would speed our spiritual progress. I could never practice the "reveal Thyself" mantra for any length of time, because deep inside there came an answer: "I have revealed Myself. I have revealed Myself in creation."

In the spring of 1997, with Easter approaching, I felt more freedom to meditate on Jesus. At this point, when I tried the "reveal Thyself" mantra, an additional answer came in my heart: "I have given you words to live by, and I am revealed in Jesus." I found that my meditations on Jesus were of a far different quality than the usual kriya yoga I normally practiced. Despite the extraordinary bliss I had previously experienced in kriya meditation, there was something more desirable about Jesus. I wasn't purposely trying to compare kriya meditation to Jesus, but when I began to meditate on Jesus and His life I was connecting with Someone real, true, and secure.

Our observance of the Easter holiday demonstrated that the inconsistency I had noticed in the ashram toward Christianity actually extended to Jesus Himself. The preparations for Easter were similar to those for the observance of special days associated with the gurus. For example, for the gurus' birthdays, we prepared special flower sashes and festoons for their photographs and the altars. We had special meals and special meditation sessions, in which the words and teachings of the particular guru would be featured. At the end of the meditation, each nun would approach the decorated picture of the particular guru with hands held in a pranam so that she could bow to the ground before the picture, then back away in obeisance. The Easter celebration was similar in all respects except one. Instead of Jesus' words and teachings being featured during the meditation, it was the guru's words and teachings *about* Jesus—quite a difference. I noticed the difference but didn't ask anyone the reason for it. I had learned not to question such things. Instead, I continued my secret practice of meditating on Jesus, although not every day. Even though I was uncomfortable with the inconsistencies at the ashram, I nevertheless wanted to succeed there, and that required consistent practice of kriya yoga meditation.

Changes on the Horizon

There was a new development in the spring of 1997 during the time in which my housemother was isolated because of her health. The personnel office instructed me to make medical and dental appointments. Such instructions were usually a sign that a nun was being considered for the novice vow, as the organization wanted all medical and dental problems remedied before it took on financial responsibility for the novice. I welcomed the prospect of being considered for the novice vow, but I also wanted to see a physician for a more immediate need—I could hardly breathe.

After several delays, I eventually saw the physician in the summer. My condition was no mystery to the doctor. She diagnosed asthma, secondary to allergies. She advised me to eliminate all allergens from my diet and environment. To do so, I would have to move from the PA, where there were two dogs, and be permitted to deviate from the central kitchen's main menu.

The Heart-*Changer*

The director of personnel made these changes as soon as she learned of my problem. I moved across the street to a house that served as the nursing home for elderly nuns, although a few younger nuns on active duty lived there as well. There were no pets, and I could cook my own food.

My housemother and I could communicate only by letter because of her isolation. She was very upset that I had been diagnosed with asthma and was now separated from the postulant routine. Somebody had to take the blame for this turn of events, and that was me. In her view, if I had simply shared my problem with her, all these serious ramifications could have been avoided. It was during this interchange that she admitted that the personnel department had lost my file soon after I'd entered. I protested that if they had told me earlier, I could have filled out the forms again, and they would have known of my allergies. So, how was I to blame?

With my unforgiving spirit still intact, fully loaded, and ready to fire, I seethed with anger toward my housemother because she had been instrumental in the problem, yet now she shifted the entire blame to me. I boiled when I remembered how I had tried to explain my problems to her several times before, but had been told that I had no choice but to conform or leave. I had suffered for months, and my entire ashram experience up to that point had been all but ruined, all because of her. And what was her defense? She explained that she had acted out of "divine love."

When I received her explanation, something extraordinary happened. Seemingly out of nowhere, I remembered two Bible verses that I didn't even know I knew. Perhaps I had learned them as a child in Sunday school, or maybe I had read them that summer during law school, but I had no specific memory of a time in my life when they had been meaningful. The first was, "Greater love hath no man than this, that a man lay down his life for his friends," which is John 15:13. The second was, "By their fruits ye shall know them," which is Matthew 7:20. These verses were, in a way, like a splash of cold water on my face. It was if I was suddenly awakened—but it was still my old angry self that awakened. In my judgmental mind, I wondered how anyone who loved me, especially someone who claimed to act out of divine love, could have misled me for months. This course of action was unacceptable, and I had been the victim. This one offense stirred up all the old, unforgiven offenses and emotional wounds in my heart. Once more, I faced the bitterness oozing just beneath the surface, ready to erupt.

I contemplated the question of "what love really would have done" for several days, trying to formulate a response to my housemother. At first, I was trying to compose a cold reply that was biting yet tactful—so that I could unleash my bitter anger yet avoid being disciplined. I rationalized my vengeful motive, thinking, "Even the kind of love that comes with common decency would never have done to me what she's done." The more I wrote, the more I realized that, even though I was suddenly able to discern between what love would do and what it wouldn't, I couldn't even forgive my housemother. When I stopped to be honest with myself, I realized the treatment I had received from her was well-deserved in light of the way I had treated others in the past. I knew I had not lived a life of love. I deserved to die for the way I had treated others, and I was now as incapable of love as ever. My seething anger was proof enough.

My body was extremely weak because of the asthma, as my lung capacity had dwindled to less than one-half. I was also suffering from daily migraines without treatment. But worse than the physical suffering was the condemnation I felt. The weight of the present circumstances, as well as all of my past, bore down on me heavily.

In my fatigue and pain, I evaluated the situation. I had done everything I had been asked to do and followed all instructions to the best of my ability. I had meditated more and more, and always more. It seemed as if perhaps I should have earned a little grace, but none was forthcoming. Nothing in the guru's teachings offered any comfort or solution. My housemother, the guru's channel, opposed me. All was lost. I had failed at everything, especially in changing myself.

Little did I know that it would be at this very time that God would begin to reveal true grace to me, and that He would pour it out in such abundance that my life would never be the same.

Chapter Four

~ ~ ~

Nothing Less

Being isolated from the other postulants was essential to my physical survival, but it changed the dynamics between us drastically. I was no longer really a part of them, even though I mirrored their schedule as best I could. I saw them at times when they were not in the PA itself, but things were very different. Once again, I was an outsider, not fitting in anywhere in the ashram social structure.

But I tried to make the best of living in the elderly nuns' house. Being fond of elderly people anyway, I enjoyed interacting with them, and we tried to cheer each other up. Plus, there were advantages to living there. I had a private room and a portable air filter with a fan loud enough to cover all other noise, and I gained much physical relief by eating meals I'd prepared.

One of the younger nuns, a novice who also lived there, showed compassion toward me. She advised me to ignore what anyone else said or did, and just go my own way, so long as I did not violate any of the rules. She gave me a *Guidepost* magazine to read, telling me in her thick Portuguese accent, "It is good magazine and will help you." I appreciated her help, but by that time I had become so accustomed to the structure of ashram life that it was difficult to take much comfort in independence. There was nothing but uncertainty in my future. I didn't know what was expected of me anymore or whether I would even be allowed to stay.

The Heart-*Changer*

One day shortly after I had moved, I was at my desk in the correspondence department, ignoring the letters in front of me and feeling crushed beneath a burden of condemnation and hopelessness. Sitting on one side of my desk was a 16 by 20 picture of the guru. In days past, I had loved this picture. It had captured my fascination and devotion daily as I had looked into the guru's eyes, but it offered no consolation at this point. Instead my attention was on a one inch sticky note on a shelf in the middle of my desk. On it, I had written a word that had welled up in my heart, a word I had remembered from several years before in my study of Hebrew: "chesed," which means God's merciful lovingkindness.[1] This word was my only comfort as I sat there under the crushing spiritual burden. I cried out to God in my heart for *chesed*, unable to hold back the tears.

A great conflict was boiling within me. My life in the ashram was in shambles. Was this disaster just a test of my loyalty and devotion to the guru? Was this, the guru's test, my "dark night of the soul"? Or was the whole thing a fraud to begin with? Any time I had a doubt about the guru, his teachings, or his ashram, I was immediately overcome with guilt, fear, and anxiety. Yet, when I tried to plunge into his teachings, I found nothing but emptiness. I kept up with meditation, but felt no devotion. I was merely going through the motions.

Back at my room, I received a note from my housemother that she wanted to see me. She told me to come to her room at a certain time to discuss my situation and the letters I had sent her, in which I'd essentially requested that she leave me alone until I could pull myself together. I wasn't ready to see her. She was in isolation because of chemotherapy, and her health was in a delicate state. I was still dealing with my unforgiving spirit, and I didn't want my anger and resentment to vent towards her, possibly even affecting her health. I didn't trust my self-control. My dilemma was that if I obeyed her command to go to her room, I would likely hurt her; but if I disobeyed and did not go,

Chapter Four

I would be insubordinate. She demanded that I see her and set the appointment.

The conflict in me raged on, but rather than obey my housemother blindly, I turned for guidance to my small children's Bible, the one I had brought from home. It was really just the New Testament with Psalms and Proverbs in the back. By no means was it my habit to consult the Bible for guidance; I only opened it up randomly when I felt deeply troubled. Groping for something that felt safe, I reached for it, and it happened to open to Psalm 119, where I read:

> O how I love thy law! It is my meditation all the day.
> Thou through thy commandments hast made me wiser than mine enemies:
> for they are ever with me.
> I have more understanding than all my teachers:
> for thy testimonies are my meditation.
> I understand more than the ancients, because I keep thy precepts.
> I have refrained my feet from every evil way, that I might keep thy word.
> I have not departed from thy judgments: for thou hast taught me.
> How sweet are thy words to my taste! Yea, sweeter than honey to my mouth!
> Through thy precepts I get understanding; therefore I hate every false way.

Each verse burst with significance in my heart, giving me assurance that by not obeying my housemother I was following the right way, a wiser way than my "teachers" were telling me. But the last line, especially, pierced through me to the core. "I hate every false way." I immediately knew that I was involved in a "false way," but it was a knowing that was very deep inside. At the time, I didn't want to accept it, yet I couldn't let go of it. It would take quite a bit more time before this knowing would become a settled, sure knowing that I would accept.

But I knew that I should not go to my housemother's room as she had ordered, and this instruction I could accept. It just wasn't right, at least not yet. I had to avoid a confrontation. So, I didn't go. I missed the appointment and thereby disobeyed a direct order from my superior. I wondered what the consequences would be. But the new knowledge that I was involved in a false way distracted me from worry over my disobedience. I could think of little else.

The next day in the correspondence department, I took the large Bible from the reference shelf to my desk and looked in the concordance for references to "antichrist." A question had arisen in my mind since reading Psalm 119, and I had to know: "If I am involved with a false way, is the guru the 'antichrist'?" I looked up the references and found in First John 4:3, "And every spirit that confesseth not that Jesus Christ is come in the flesh is not of God: and this is the spirit of antichrist, whereof ye have heard that it should come; and even now already is it in the world." It didn't seem from this verse that the guru was "the" antichrist, but it dawned on me that if the spirit of antichrist was already in the world at the time the Bible was written, then it surely is here now. I wondered even more whether I was involved with such a spirit of antichrist. I was very troubled, but I tried to maintain a cool composure outwardly. I didn't want the other nuns to know the nature or depth of my inward struggle.

In the midst of this inner turmoil, something happened that brought me hope and strength to go on. A hymn came to mind. I probably hadn't heard it since I was a teenager, but the words and music came back to my memory:

My hope is built on nothing less
Than Jesus' blood and righteousness.
I dare not trust the sweetest frame,
But wholly lean on Jesus' name.

Chapter Four

On Christ, the solid Rock, I stand.
All other ground is sinking sand,
All other ground is sinking sand.[2]

I had no idea what these words really meant. I just knew that when I sang them silently in my mind they gave me comfort—the only comfort I had. With this song in my heart, I felt I could make it. So, as I walked the tree-lined street of the ashram, I was mentally singing, "My hope is built on nothing less than Jesus' blood and righteousness . . . On Christ, the solid Rock, I stand, all other ground is sinking sand . . . ." Nobody else knew. Or so I thought.

One evening, perhaps a day or two after I began relying on this hymn for strength, I was in my room just after dusk, reading the *Guidepost* magazine and feeling calm. The air filter was on, and I wasn't experiencing any asthma symptoms at all. I could breathe normally and deeply. Everything was peaceful. In fact, I was thinking how the simple faith of the Christians presented in the articles seemed "like a breath of fresh air" compared to the confusion I'd experienced at the ashram. Suddenly, an invisible force began to choke me. It was as if there was a pair of unseen hands around my neck, strangling me. I stood up and tried to move toward the door, but could not. After thirty seconds or so, I don't know how I knew, but somehow I knew the only way to stop this attack was to begin to say, "Krishna, Krishna, Krishna . . . ." As I coughed out the name of this other god, the invisible hands let go. But I felt a lingering threat, one that was not soon forgotten.

As for human hands, I was never officially punished for missing the appointment with my housemother. At first I was relieved. I had expected discipline from the personnel department but never received any communication from anyone other than my housemother herself a few days, perhaps a week, later. She expressed her extreme disappointment in me, but I was not

The Heart-Changer

reprimanded in any other way. The correction would prove to be more subtle and more permanent.

After her note to me, my housemother and I exchanged correspondence for a few days, sharing our perspectives. Eventually I did meet with her in her room one evening after dusk, in the darkness. She never turned on the light. It would be the last time I would talk with her in person as a resident of the ashram, although I didn't know it.

Part of the discussion that evening concerned the biannual renewal of my law license in Ohio, which had been an ongoing topic for several months. She informed me that the organization wanted me to renew as an active attorney in Ohio, rather than on inactive status as previously discussed, because there was no guarantee how long I would be staying at the ashram. I began to get the hint.

Within a few days, my brother called with the news that I was needed at home because my mother had been hospitalized. I received permission to leave the ashram for a short time, but I packed all my important papers and nearly all my clothes.

On August 24, 1997, I awoke about 4:00 a.m. to get dressed and gather my things. I left the ashram that Sunday morning, in the darkness.

The Long Battle

My brother picked me up at the airport two hours away from my hometown in Ohio. On the ride home, I learned that my mother had already been released from the hospital. I asked him why he had told me she was so ill, but he said he didn't remember saying it. What a mystery! Yet, I didn't even care to solve it. More pressing matters were on my mind—the turmoil and confusion within me.

Leaving the ashram did little to relieve the inner turmoil. With the choking incident, as well as other things I had seen, I discerned a spiritual darkness there, and I wanted far away

Chapter Four

from it. But, being grounded in the guru's teachings, I feared the consequences of leaving. Also, my pride was sorely hurt. It was so hard to give in to the perceived failure of leaving the ashram. Part of me wanted to prove that I could succeed there. I wanted to vindicate myself. Leaving the ashram only intensified my inner conflict.

From all outward appearances, my life fell into place quite easily and neatly during my first week back at home. My job was still waiting for me. My mother and stepfather generously gave me a new car and allowed me to stay in their home so I could save money for rent and a security deposit. On the surface, everything looked fine, but I was far from fine. The spiritual battle within me was so intense that I felt as though I was being torn apart at the atomic level.

On the one hand, it appeared as though I had been ejected, spewed out, from the ashram. Was it for my disloyalty to the guru? This thought brought much anguish. I blamed myself for doubting the guru. I wanted to quench the feeling of rejection by returning to the ashram. I thought of all the wonderful aspects of the guru's teachings—love, joy, peace. How could anything so good be bad? On the other hand, how could I ignore the darkness I'd seen, the choking incident, and the warning that the guru's way was a false way? Confusion was tearing me apart.

After a week or ten days, my housemother called to make arrangements for shipping the rest of my belongings. I asked about the possibility of returning, either in the near future or at any time, ever. She informed me that this option was not available. This news was a hard blow.

I tried to contact one senior nun who had offered me sympathy during my last month or so at the ashram, but when I called her she reminded me that to stay in contact would constitute a friendship. Monastic disciples were not to cultivate friendships with anyone, but focus only on their relationship with God and guru. But I *had* developed friendships with the women there. We all had developed friendships with one another. It was a cloistered environment, and the nuns were the only people with whom I had interacted for nineteen months. With all contact severed, I felt very alone.

The rejection resurrected all the old feelings festering inside me from earlier in life. The weight and pain of it all was agonizing.

I felt utterly abandoned by God. Meditation was out of the question. I simply hurt too badly. Instead, I took long walks on the rural roads around my stepfather's house, and at times the pain and rejection came out in a sobbing, convulsing prayer: "Why don't You want me? Why don't You want me?" (I had no idea what was transpiring in the spiritual realm on my behalf.)

A couple of times, when my mother and stepfather were gone, I turned on a Christian television station. Some of the programs were very insightful. The speakers seemed to have answers to some of the most pressing questions I had struggled with at the ashram, such as, "Why can't I change myself?" Then, as if coming to my senses, when I remembered my pledge of loyalty to the guru, I would say to myself, "Why should I listen to these people? They are not even God-realized masters," and turn off the television.

One day, I saw on the front page of the local newspaper a large color photo of several smiling couples who had just returned from Russia. It captured my attention, both because the beaming couples looked so peaceful and satisfied, and because one of the couples looked familiar. As I read the caption underneath, I learned that the familiar-looking ones were parents of a grade school classmate. I knew these people were Christians. They had just returned from a mission trip. But it was not the fact that they had been to Russia on a mission trip that impressed me. I must have stared at their picture for ten minutes, because in their faces I saw genuine peace and joy, such as I had not seen at the ashram. In my heart, I knew they had something I desired more than anything.

Chapter Four

After about a month, I had enough money to rent an apartment in the same complex I had lived in before going to the ashram. I furnished it with sturdy, plastic lawn furniture, which I bought at an end-of-the-season sale. Yes, my apartment had an ascetic quality, but I found that the white plastic Adirondack chair and ottoman were as comfortable place as any, so long as I put a roll of paper towels behind my neck to cushion my head. Needless to say, I didn't entertain guests. My concern, however, was not with a social life, but only with my quest. Once and for all, what is the truth?

An old friend who had tried to talk me out of going to the ashram in the first place gave me a study Bible containing practical, life application footnotes. This Bible was in a modern English version, much easier to read than the King James Version I'd always encountered before. So I began reading it more.

But at the same time, I decided to go back to the basics with the guru. I went back to the beginning lessons to study them all over again, and I redoubled my efforts in reading the guru's books. As my housemother had patterned her life after St. Therese of Lisieux, I decided to read some writings of Catholic saints as well.

I wasted no time with entertainment. I owned no television. I worked, but when I wasn't at work I was trying to find the truth.

Each day was a new battle, fought in every sphere of life—physical, emotional, and spiritual. I was in constant pain in each. The physical pain was such that at times I wondered whether I was relapsing into chronic fatigue syndrome—except that I wasn't fatigued. I was experiencing a painful, nervous energy so that I couldn't relax or find relief in anything but kriya yoga. Only by doing kriyas could I relieve the pain.

But when I tried to meditate, I knew overwhelmingly that Jesus didn't want me doing kriya. Somehow I knew that Jesus didn't want me even to sing the same chants I had at the ashram. I felt immense pressure and conflict. Considering my physical pain and fear of the consequences for being disloyal to the guru, it is a fair statement that my decision to stop practicing kriya yoga meditation was a monumental one. Instead of meditating as usual, I sang a new, simple song that I made up to these words I'd found in the Bible: "The Lord is good, His mercy endures forever." Then I simply sat in silence.

But there was little respite from feeling torn apart by the spiritual conflict. At times, it seemed as if it would never end.

Longing for a more "spiritual environment," I sometimes went to Christian bookstores. I found tapes of Bible verses set to music in beautiful arrangements. These were a comfort, so I played them often, and the word of God began to filter down into my heart.

One of the earliest tapes I purchased had an arrangement of Proverbs 3:5-6: "Trust in the Lord with all your heart, and lean not on your own understanding. In all your ways acknowledge Him, and He shall direct your paths" (NKJV). Another had Psalm 138:7-8: "Though I walk in the midst of trouble, You will revive me; You will stretch out Your hand against the wrath of my enemies, and Your right hand will save me. The Lord will perfect that which concerns me; Your mercy, O Lord, endures forever; do not forsake the works of Your hands" (NKJV). When I sang these verses along with the tapes, I found assurance that God was caring for me.

Also, I seemed to find verses in the Bible at just the right time. I found hope when I first read Psalm 51. Under the burden of such condemnation I had felt for so long, it was like water to a parched mouth to read this:

> Have mercy on me, O God, according to Your unfailing love;
> According to Your great compassion, blot out my transgressions.
> Wash away all my iniquity and cleanse me from my sin.

Chapter Four

> For I know my transgressions, and my sin is always before me.
> Against You, You only, have I sinned, and done what is evil in Your sight,
> So that You are proved right when You speak and justified when You judge...
> Surely You desire truth in the inner parts;
> You teach me wisdom in the inmost place...
> Cleanse me with hyssop, and I will be clean.
> Wash me, and I will be whiter than snow...
> Create in me a pure heart, O God...
> You do not delight in sacrifice, or I would bring it;
> You do not take pleasure in burnt offerings.
> The sacrifices of God are a broken and contrite spirit;
> A broken and contrite heart, O God, You will not despise. . . .

All I had to offer was a broken heart and a willingness to let go of my inner defenses. Slowly, I was able to let down the wall around my heart a little to feel the brokenness.

But even prayer was a battle, because in order to pray one must know to whom one is praying. The God of the Bible, about whom I was reading and learning, was so very different from the one described by the guru. When I read Psalm 86:5, "For You, Lord, are good, and ready to forgive, and abundant in mercy to all who call upon You," it was clear that it was not referring to a deity who requires a person to rid herself of bad karma through reincarnation, or a deity who must be coaxed through mantras to give attention to a devotee, or a deity who makes truth available only to a select few. Yet when I tried to pray, my thoughts would become jumbled with the issue of loyalty to the guru, and doubts would arise. Eventually I began to say aloud, "I am praying to the God of Abraham, of Isaac, and of Jacob. I am praying to the

God who is the Father of Jesus Christ, the God of the Bible." Then my thoughts would settle, and I could pray.

When I read Psalm 86:11, "Unite my heart, that I may fear Your name," it became my prayer. I wanted a heart that was no longer divided, but united in truth. I wanted a heart to know God.

The problem was that as I read books by the guru and his closest followers, I found many good things. They said many of the same things that the Catholic saints had said about making an effort to please God, especially in the monastic life. The guru had written about love, prayer, faith, kindness, the Golden Rule, practicing the presence of God, persevering under difficult circumstances, and leaving results to God. Undeniably, it is true that if one could consistently practice these teachings, one would likely become a better person, because much of what the guru taught is from the Bible. This apparent similarity was a source of confusion. Again I was faced with the perplexing question: "How could something so good be bad?"

In one of the early lessons the guru taught about forgiving others, especially as a means of freedom for oneself. This truth had resonated within me because of my past experiences, but I had never stopped to think the issue through as I should have: If forgiving others is the right thing to do, and if it brings spiritual freedom, then how is it that the god about whom the guru taught does not forgive humans their transgressions, but rather requires them to work out bad karma in many, many incarnations? How could such a god be spiritually free? How could God require more of us humans than He is willing to do Himself? These questions had never entered my mind before. I had followed the guru without question, really, because of the blissful experiences. Now that I was out of the ashram, such questions actually caused me pain, literal physical suffering. The more I doubted the guru, the more physical and spiritual agony I felt.

But the more I read the Bible, the more there was to doubt about the guru. I began reading the specific verses he used to "prove" his points, but I read them in context. For example, the guru quoted a particular verse to support his claim that Jesus taught about the "spiritual eye" which could be seen in kriya yoga meditation. The verse was Matthew 6:22: "The light of the body is the eye; if therefore thine eye be single, thy whole body shall be full of light." The guru said that Jesus was talking about the single spiritual eye a devotee sees when she has become completely calm in meditation. But when I read the entire chapter before and after the verse, it was obvious that the guru's interpretation was far-fetched. The same was true for other quotations he used. When I read the chapter before and the chapter after such verses, I found that the meaning the guru had attributed to them simply did not hold true.

On one memorable occasion, I found Ephesians 6:12, and read, "For our struggle is not against flesh and blood, but against the rulers, against the authorities, against the powers of this dark world and against the spiritual forces of evil in the heavenly realms." The concept of spiritual forces of evil in heavenly realms shocked me. For so long as I had been with the guru, I had not given a single thought to discerning between good and evil spiritual forces. Anything spiritual was assumed to be good among the guru's devotees, and the same had been true for me until I read this verse.

Soon after, I found 2 Corinthians 11:13-14: "For such men are false apostles, deceitful workmen, masquerading as apostles of Christ. And no wonder, for Satan himself masquerades as an angel of light." This new knowledge truly frightened me. Satan as an angel of light? Could it be? Had my blissful experiences been brought about by evil spiritual forces, or by Satan himself disguised as an angel of light?

The more I questioned the guru, the more painful my life became. Once again, merely breathing was difficult at times, although there were no allergens in my apartment to cause asthma attacks. There was a constant, oppressive heaviness in my chest and abdomen. At times my entire body felt as if it would either explode or implode. The battle raged on, and I was the battlefield.

My Feet in Both Camps

As Christmas approached, I decided to make cards for each nun at the ashram. I wanted to send my greetings, but I also wanted them to remember me. As was the custom at the ashram, I crafted each card by hand.

I received Christmas greetings from the ashram also, quite unexpectedly. On Christmas Eve, my former housemother called with the news that the personnel department had decided I could re-enter the ashram under certain conditions. I would need to be debt-free with at least ten thousand dollars in savings, and I would have to undergo counseling for emotional immaturity. Upon my fulfilling these conditions, the organization would hire me as an employee to work under the nuns' supervision for a year or so before I could re-enter as a nun. I thanked her profusely! I was undaunted by the conditions, even though I knew the financial requirements would take years to accomplish. I asked my housemother to forgive me for the unkind things I must have said and the petulant attitude I must have displayed during my time at the ashram. She very kindly said that she didn't even think of those things anymore, and that I shouldn't think of them either.

That Christmas Eve, I went to a candlelight service at a local church and sang carols joyously, thanking God and guru for their mercy in accepting me again. Returning home, I slept on the floor, as was my custom, but this night by my "Christmas tree"—a string of colored lights coiled on a sheet of aluminum foil—happy and content.

Days later, however, my inward battle raged again. How could I forget all that had happened at the ashram, all the darkness I had seen? How could I trust the guru now? No, I was more determined than ever to find the truth.

Chapter Four

Moreover, there was a new emotional dimension added to my torment, caused once again by my unforgiving spirit. As the implications of the conditions for re-entry clarified in my mind, my anger toward my housemother returned. She had again placed all the blame on me—on my emotional immaturity. Pride and indignation rose to the surface as I inwardly boiled, protesting, "How would years of counseling for me change the facts and events as they happened? She says she's sorry for her mistake, but she doesn't really accept the blame!" I had never truly forgiven her for the shortcomings I perceived in her, no matter how many times I said I had. And my bitter anger was making me miserable, as always.

Despite my anger, I took her advice and began seeing a professional counselor. Following my housemother's instructions was a way to keep all my options open. It seemed as if I my heart was connecting more with the Bible than ever, but I just wasn't sure. I wasn't willing or able to commit myself exclusively to Jesus or the guru. I wasn't willing to make a decision once and for all because I feared being wrong.

Such was my state at the beginning of 1998. I was no longer confined behind steel bars and gates, but I still wasn't free. Oh, I wanted more than ever to be free—especially from the inner conflict. But I still didn't truly know what I needed freedom *from*. I wanted a clean heart, but still clung to pride and a judgmental attitude. The newly-reactivated lava of bitterness from my unforgiving spirit caused all the resentment against all those who had ever "hurt me" to overflow. I was in intense physical and spiritual suffering most, if not all, the time. I didn't realize the extent to which I was at a crossroads. I only knew it was an agonizing place to be.

But there was a new, positive factor that made an enormous difference. A few weeks before Christmas, a couple had come to my office for a new will. They were cheerful, pleasant people, and they asked if I was enjoying the season, listening to Christmas music and such. I told them I didn't have any recordings of

The Heart-*Changer*

Christmas songs. Before they left, they gave me the dial number for a radio station that was playing Christmas music continually through the month of December.

I developed a habit of listening to this station while making cards for the nuns, doing housekeeping, and driving. It was a Christian station. After the holidays, the radios in my apartment and car were still tuned to it, and I began to listen to some of the teaching programs. At first, I reacted the same way I had to Christian television shows months earlier. Out of fear of disloyalty to the guru, I asked, "Why should I listen to these people who are not even God-realized masters?" But slowly, I gained courage to listen to entire programs.

By mid-January, I rationalized that it was the guru's utter humility to step aside and let me fall in love with Jesus completely, so it was all right for me to do so. But because I was loving Jesus, yet praising the guru for allowing this to happen—so that I could be loyal to him—the battle continued. One cannot serve two masters.

By the end of January, I felt so overwhelmed that I had to write a list of questions to sort through my conflict: "Am I confusing my strong emotional reaction to the treatment I received at the ashram with the question of whether I should be loyal to the guru? Why should I 'go against God' by being disloyal to the guru just because of my hurt feelings? Aren't my hurt feelings just a sign of the emotional immaturity the guru's channel has diagnosed? Wasn't such treatment just an example of the guru's method of, 'I will hurt you until you can hurt no longer,' that is, until you die to your little self and give up this delusive dream? And if I question this treatment, doesn't it show my lack of humility and loyalty? Isn't disloyalty the 'highest sin,' according to the guru? Didn't St. Teresa of Avila write, 'Do you want only reasonable crosses'? What about the chela incident? Was this Satan? How could it be? The moments when I accepted discipline by the guru were good, but the moments of doubting are turmoil and pain—so, in reality my doubts are terrible and satanic—aren't they?"

I wrote these questions rapidly as they came to mind. But as I reviewed them more slowly, I still felt the only safe place was with Jesus. I also felt deficient and flawed. If my doubts were coming from Satan, then I felt he had won the battle. I was too agonized and too numb, too much at conflict and lacking in strength or faith to be of any value.

Then, with surprising insight I recorded this question: "Does Satan use the hurt from the past to sow doubt and separation from God in the present?" This insight, I later would realize, was directly from God.

The final question I recorded was, "Whose disciple am I?"— for I knew I was a disciple of someone.

I decided to search for truth by testing the veracity of the guru's teachings using non-biblical sources, thinking, "If the teachings are factual, then I'll know I can trust him and that my doubts are wrong. But if he lied, then why should I be loyal to him?" I chose one portion of the guru's teachings that seemed central to my quest: one footnote from his autobiography in which he claimed that reincarnation was an accepted doctrine taught in "original Christianity." He wrote that Origen, an early church father, had taught reincarnation, but that all references to it were erased from church doctrine at the Second Council of Constantinople in 553 A.D. I researched at both the local library and a university library, where I read everything I could find on Origen and the Second Council of Constantinople. I found Origen's writings on the internet and read them (a difficult task). Origen had written about the pre-existence of the soul, a concept he borrowed from Plato. His work was heavily influenced by Greek philosophy, and in this respect was not true to the Hebrew origins of Christianity. I found nothing to support the guru's claim that Origen wrote about or believed in reincarnation, or that reincarnation was a doctrine of "original Christianity." And most certainly, I found nothing to support the guru's claim that Jesus Himself taught reincarnation. The guru had lied. As I accepted this conclusion, my daily physical and spiritual pain increased.

As of the beginning of February 1998, I had endured five months of this intense battle. The closer I moved toward Jesus, the more pain I suffered, especially the heaviness in my chest and abdomen. Also, the constant nervous energy in my muscles was becoming all but unbearable. Still resisting the urge to do kriya meditation for relief, I had to keep moving constantly so as not to succumb to the pain and agitation. When I wasn't working or reading, I went to the high school track to walk—and walk and walk and walk—even in the cold weather. I felt as if I would burst apart at times, and I wondered how much longer I could exist this way.

It was as if the guru were just behind my shoulder, saying, "Just do one kriya, and it will all go away. Just one kriya, and all will be well. You'll be fine again." He was holding my body hostage.

One day in mid-February as I was walking around the track alone, half praying for relief and half crying, the thought occurred to me, "I will not give up seeking the truth just to escape how I feel. I will not decide *anything* based on how I feel!" I stopped walking, planted my feet firmly, pointed my finger in front of me and stated forcefully, aloud, "I don't care if you make me feel this way for the rest of my life! If it comes between choosing you and choosing Jesus, I choose Jesus!" Immediately, the pain and agony lifted. My body relaxed, and I could breathe deeply. There was a soothing peace in my chest and abdomen as I stood there and slowly took in the fact that he who had tormented me was gone. "Thank You, Jesus," I whispered.

My journal reflects a change as of this event. Up to this day, the entries had included quotations from the guru and his followers, as well as from non-biblical and New Age channeling sources, along with quotations from the Bible. I had written prayers to the guru as well as prayers to Jesus. But after this event on the track, I quoted and considered only Bible verses, and my prayers were only to the God of the Bible—only about Jesus.

My questions took on a different form. Since returning from the ashram, the primary issue had been my pledge of loyalty and obedience to the guru. Because it was now clear that the guru had been untruthful, and that some spiritual power associated with him had actually tortured me for months, my fear of being disloyal was well on the way to being overcome by my discovery of safety in Jesus. The questions in my heart, then, were the same ones that had been there for many years before I'd known about the guru—questions that were so heart-rending that I had suppressed them, yet deeply yearned for their answers: "What do I have to do to get God to love me? Will He ever accept me? How can I please Him? And how can I change myself?"

I began to write out passages from the Bible in an attempt to grasp their meaning:

> If we claim to be without sin, we deceive ourselves and the truth is not in us. If we confess our sins, He is faithful and just to forgive us our sins and purify us from all unrighteousness (1 John 1:8-9).

> Therefore, since we have been justified through faith, we have peace with God through our Lord Jesus Christ, through whom we have gained access by faith into this grace in which we now stand (Rom. 5:1-2).

> You see, at just the right time, when we were still powerless, Christ died for the ungodly. Very rarely will anyone die for a righteous man, though for a good man someone might possibly dare to die. But God demonstrates His own love for us

in this: while we were still sinners, Christ died for us (Rom. 5:5-8).

Never in my life had I understood the significance of the death of Jesus Christ. As a child, my reaction to hearing about Jesus' death was that it was just one more thing to feel guilty about, since I felt guilty for my very existence. Through the years I had tried so many ways to find some meaning in life: music, career, relationships, and religion, to name a few. Despite all I'd tried, I'd never found the answer to the question, "What do I have to do to get God to love me?" Further, my heart told me I was not really worthy of God's love. I didn't even like myself, so how could He love me? I had tried so hard to change, to become a better person and do good things, but I had always failed.

On a trip to a Christian bookstore I found a laminated bookmark with verses listed under various headings. Hoping these might help, I bought the bookmark and wrote out these verses:

> But your iniquities have separated you from your God; your sins have hidden His face from you, so that He will not hear (Is. 59:2).
>
> All of us have become like one who is unclean, and all our righteous acts are like filthy rags (Is. 64:6).
>
> For all have sinned and fall short of the glory of God (Rom. 3:23).
>
> For the wages of sin is death, but the gift of God is eternal life in Christ Jesus our Lord (Rom. 6:23).

For the first time I began to grasp the concept that there is a God who offers salvation and acceptance as a gift, not as something I could earn, or was expected to earn, by being a good person. If

Chapter Four

God's forgiveness and acceptance could come to me as a gift—if I could really trust this—it was certainly good news. After all, I knew from years of experience that all my sincerest efforts at becoming acceptable had never worked. And I knew the utter hopelessness of trying to counteract every bad act or attitude with an equally good or better one.

From roughly mid-February to mid-March, a teacher on the Christian radio station ran a series of programs featuring discussions on whether salvation was by grace or by works. I made a point to listen each day, and the issue became better-formulated in my mind. It became clear that there was no such thing as a hybrid of grace and works. Grace is grace—a free gift, which is completely unearned and unmerited. And it also became clear that the Bible teaches that God's salvation is by grace, not works. "What a concept," I thought, "salvation by grace."

I had been attending a nearby church for several weeks, but was unimpressed each week by the lax attitude of the people there. In contrast to the nuns at the ashram, who always sat in complete silence with backs ramrod straight before services, the atmosphere at the church was more like a basketball or football game. In fact, much of the pre-service and pre-Sunday school chit-chat focused on high school sports, which seemed trivial to me. After I gained the revelation that salvation was by grace, it bothered me even more that everyone at the church was so casual about being there. I thought, "If these Christians really believe salvation is by grace, they should be leaping for joy."

By mid-March, in my mind at least, I had made a decision—an almost firm decision. I was confident that the Bible was true, and that the guru's interpretation of it was not. I was confident that Jesus was safe, and that I was His. I knew the guru was not safe, and I didn't want to be his.

In light of this decision, I had the unrealistic expectation that I would change. I thought my behavior and attitudes would improve. But each day, for one reason or another, I was disappointed in myself, perhaps for unkindness or gossip, or for

The Heart-*Changer*

having to force myself to do something good rather than doing it from the heart.

I had found First John 3:16-23:

> This is how we know what love is: Jesus Christ laid down His life for us. And we ought to lay down our lives for our brothers. If anyone has material possessions and sees his brother in need but has no pity on him, how can the love of God be in him? Dear children, let us not love with words or tongue, but with actions and in truth. This then is how we know that we belong to the truth, and how we set our hearts at rest in His presence whenever our hearts condemn us. For God is greater than our hearts, and He knows everything. Dear friends, if our hearts do not condemn us, we have confidence before God and receive from Him everything we ask, because we obey His commands and do what pleases Him. And this is His command: to believe in the name of His Son, Jesus Christ, and to love one another as He commanded us.

My heart certainly condemned me, because I truly had little or no ability to give or receive love.

Also by mid-March, my counselor recommended that I discontinue the sessions—not because I was all better, but because I never would be! She said that she was pleased by how hard I was working at "reframing" the issues from my past, but the process would be life-long. At best, perhaps I would be able to have a little happiness occasionally. The psychological prognosis was official: I could expect minimal happiness *if* I tried my very best. My past would always rule my future.

Then around March 20th, the guru, or the demon-spirit behind him, hit me full force again. All of the physical pain, the spiritual agony, and the emotional anxiety returned, and once again I felt as if I were being torn apart at the atomic level. And just as before, except even more strongly, it was as if the spirit of the guru was over my shoulder saying, "Just one kriya, just one kriya, and it will all go away."

In the previous months, even though I had been going through much turmoil, I was able to maintain a façade of composure at work. With this renewed attack, the mask came off and, in a shocking display, I showed vehement anger toward a secretary at the law office. Then, I was ashamed. The feeling of condemnation was crushing. So, I ran out and bought a self-help book on how to control anger.

I knew I had to pull myself together. For one thing, I had an interview for a new job the next day. Based on the information in my new book, I rationalized, "This anger is an autonomic physical response, and kriya will take care of that." The morning of the interview, Saturday, March 21, 1998, in order to calm myself, I did five kriyas.

I knew that it was wrong—dark. I knew that Jesus did not want me to do the kriyas. But I did them anyway. Strangely, it was as if He did not condemn me.

After the interview, I was deeply disappointed in myself. I'd placed so much importance on it that I had done something I knew full well Jesus would not like. My regret led me to reflect on the path my life had taken over the years and the motivations behind the decisions I had made. I came back to the question of why I could not truly give or receive love. Somehow in my heart I knew that in order to do so, I needed to learn how to forgive. I resolved that I wouldn't go to church the next day, but would instead spend as long as it took learning to forgive. I had a new book on the topic and was willing to do anything to change.

It completely escaped my attention that I had reached the same conclusion four years earlier on that decisive morning when I had purposely ignored the inner urging to seek out Jesus, whose way spoke of forgiveness—even forgiveness of sins. In the four

The Heart-Changer

intervening years, I had learned the futility of any other way and had cried out for mercy. After four years, I was at the same turning point.

This time the result would be different.

Chapter Five

~ ~ ~

My Day of Grace and Truth

On Sunday, March 22, 1998, I awoke and got down to business. Not taking time to eat much, or even to change out of my nightgown and bathrobe, I was determined to learn how to forgive. My instructor for the day would be the new book on forgiveness, written by one of the teachers featured on the Christian radio station.

With all my attention focused on this task and riveted on this book, I spent time grasping each concept presented. I was serious. Not a casual Sunday morning read, this was now the most important thing in my life, because I sensed that forgiving others was critically linked to the freedom and cleansing my life and heart needed so badly. As I read, I learned that forgiving is not ignoring harm done, or saying that wrongs done are really all right, but rather choosing not to hold the debt of these wrongs against the wrongdoers. The author suggested a particular method of forgiving people, whether living or dead, without actually confronting them, by sitting opposite an empty chair and imagining, one by one, each person who had caused harm. Using this method, I would "encounter" each imaginary person and release his or her debt.

All day long I remembered all the hurts I had never forgiven. I talked to the "invisible people" in the chair until I was exhausted. During breaks from this endeavor, I read other portions of the book. What I found changed my life.

The Heart-*Changer*

The author wrote about God's forgiveness, explaining how Jesus had died as *my substitute*. It was in the context of grasping Jesus as my substitute that God actually used the guru's prior deception—of my taking others' bad karma on my own body—to help me understand that Jesus could take my sin. The Bible verses I had copied during the preceding weeks came alive in my heart. I began to see it clearly: My sin would require me to suffer eternal death and separation from God. But because Jesus took the punishment and consequences for my sin on the cross, God could rightfully choose not to hold the debt of my sin against me. It was as if I had never heard this message before. If I had, I'd never understood it as I did that day. The Holy Spirit was opening my mind and heart.

Even so, I found no relief all day from the terrible burden of bitterness and unforgiveness I had carried all my life. I continued trying to forgive until that evening. By about 7:00 p.m., I had worked so hard at it that I was moist with perspiration, still in my nightclothes, as I fell exhausted into the plastic Adirondack chair. Yet, I still didn't feel that I had truly forgiven anyone. I still felt the huge burden inside—the turmoil, the unrest, the lack of peace. Would it ever end?

I closed my eyes for a moment and saw a huge, dark, cavernous, craggy pit full of filth and slime. It was a place of absolute, total pain and deep, tangible darkness. I had never seen this place before or experienced the raw revulsion of it. But somehow, in that moment, I knew the emotional pain I had felt all my life had been a shadow of its darkness spilling over into my conscious experience. It was intensely frightening. Quickly, I opened my eyes and started to get up, to get away from it.

Then I stopped and sat myself back down. "No," I thought, "you have been running from this all of your life. You are going to sit here and face it."

Once again, I closed my eyes. It was there again. Words are inadequate to describe the hopeless agony and emptiness in this thick, craggy darkness.

Chapter Five

I sat there for a few moments until I just couldn't take it any longer; then I whispered, "Lord, what is it?"

I heard a voice, not audibly, but almost. Deep within me, He said very softly and gently, "It's your sin."

At once—in the flash of an instant—I understood. Suddenly I knew that all the inner pain that all those years I thought had been caused by other people had actually been caused by my own sin—holding resentment, hatred, hostility and bitterness towards others. I knew that this pain, multiplied by millions upon millions, was what Jesus felt when He was on the cross. I gasped at the horror of it! In that instant, Jesus let me see the reality of the depth of my sin and the complete impossibility of ever escaping it myself. I cried out, "Oh! Save me!"

Then—in an instant—the burden was gone. Gone! In that moment, the darkness and pain that had plagued me for forty years was gone. I sat there quietly, and I knew, in a way that transcended any thought process, that Jesus was there with me, even though I couldn't see Him. I said, "It's You. It's really You, after all these years." Moments passed as I sat there in His presence. It was peace like I had never imagined and which can never be adequately expressed. Jesus was with me. He was within me. I talked softly with Him, and He responded deep within. It was as if He was rubbing a soothing salve on my heart. Gratitude and praise rose up inside me so intensely that the English language could not express it, and I worshiped Him in words I didn't recognize.

My life had changed in one moment, the most peaceful, loving moment I had ever known. But I had no idea of the tremendous magnitude of the change that had occurred. Little by little, I would come to understand bits and pieces of what had happened, but it would take years for me to come close to knowing its full significance.

The one thing I did understand that evening was that the painful burden was gone. But true to my lifelong habits, I told no one what had happened. For the next few days, I went about my life, secretly enjoying the peace. I was almost afraid that if I said anything about it, I would lose it.

I decided to find a church where Christians did leap for joy, at least figuratively, because of grace. After some thought, I decided to start at one point near me and move out in concentric circles, if necessary, to find a church. The next Sunday, I started one mile away at a church where the pastor taught on Second Corinthians 5:21: "God made Him who had no sin to be sin for us, so that in Him we might become the righteousness of God" (NIV). Jesus not only took my sin, but also gave me His righteousness! What grace! What marvelous grace! In his closing remarks, the pastor told anyone who had made the decision to put his or her faith in Jesus to tell somebody about it before leaving. On the way out I told him, "What you talked about today—putting faith in Jesus—I did that last week."

Then, each day seemed like a new celebration of His grace. My burden had been taken away! I was bursting with gratitude to God. Depression and despair were no longer part of my life. All my life, the weight of my own sin had been the anchor that held me in the depths of depression. I had felt as if I'd be the perpetual victim of others' unkindness, not realizing that by blaming them and holding onto bitterness I was choosing to remain a slave of despair. I had committed heinous and unloving acts against others that made my own emotional pain pale in comparison. Even worse, I had rebelled against God and consciously rejected Him. But as soon as I cried out to God for mercy, He lavished His lovingkindness on me. He didn't deal with me according to my sins. He freed me!

Being free of my burden, I was eager to release others from theirs. God had forgiven me of so much. If Jesus' death and resurrection took away my sins, then it was sufficient to take care of theirs, too. God enabled me to forgive. Now instead of guilt, I had hope!

Only two or three weeks after my new life began came the celebration of Jesus' resurrection, and for the first time in my life it would be special. At the age of forty, I was alive in Christ. I was so excited that I got up at 5:00 a.m. on Resurrection Day to make sure I would be able to watch the very first moments of daylight. I sat at the window facing the eastern sky and listened to praise music on the radio, my heart brimming over with gratitude to God for what He had done for me. That morning I heard the song, "There is a Redeemer, Jesus God's own Son, precious Lamb of God, Messiah, Holy One. . . ."[3] I wept with uncontainable praise at the realization, "There *is* a Redeemer!"

A few weeks later, the memories of my past sins started to haunt me again. I felt as if I needed to pray to God from behind a screen, so He wouldn't see me. There was no way I could look to the Holy One. Finally, on my knees, I took paper and began to list every sin I could remember. After filling two columns on the front and back, I began listing broad categories, such as wrong attitudes and spiteful feelings. Face down, I lifted the list up to God and said, "Here it is. I know You already know all this, but I just have to show You." He said, "Yes, I see, but it is gone—all taken care of." What could I say in response? No words could express my thanks. I sat in hushed and holy silence, completely sure He had forgiven my past—all of it.

Grace and Truth

I joined a Bible study at my new church in which the pastor was teaching a New Testament survey. As the weeks passed, I was amazed at the amount written in the epistles about false teachers. Written within a few decades after Jesus ascended into heaven, they warn about the false teachers who were already perverting His teachings. Some of these false teachers corrupted the truth by trying to mix grace and works—saying that faith in Jesus was not enough, but keeping the Law of Moses was also necessary to be saved. This kind of grace-works hybrid sounded all too familiar to me. And I loved the biblical response to it: Anyone who teaches this lie, let him be accursed! (See, Gal. 1:8.) There is no room for such darkness in the light of truth.

Some false teachers taught that God's grace made loose living all right. They tried to convince Christians that, since God's grace overcomes sin, then it's all right to sin more so grace can abound more (Rom. 3:8; 6:1-2). I knew this couldn't be true. God wouldn't send His Son to die for our sins just to make it possible for us to sin more. No, we aren't to use our freedom as an excuse to indulge in sin (Gal. 5:13).

Another perversion of the truth was Gnosticism, which included the false teaching of "dualism"—that the physical world is evil, and that a select few can escape to the spirit realm, the good realm, through "secret knowledge." This certainly reminded me of my former guru's teaching about escaping the rounds of reincarnation through the secret practice of kriya yoga. In early Gnosticism, false teachers taught that the divine part of Christ came upon the physical Man, Jesus, after His baptism and left Him just before He died. This, too, sounded so familiar, like the guru's teaching about "Christ-consciousness." I had fallen prey to deception that was not even new or original, but rather centuries-old false teaching in new and different packaging! No wonder the guru didn't want us to read the Bible!

Oh, how I wished I had read the Bible fully as a young person! Now, at age forty, the more I read it, the more I saw that I could have avoided so many mistakes and so much heartache. And, oh, how arrogant I had been all those years to think that I knew what the Bible said, and that I could comment on it, when in fact I had been so ignorant.

From early adolescence I had doubted the Bible's validity and accuracy, beginning with my study of evolution. My doubts had grown into full-blown rejection during my college years as I ingested the pervasive teaching about evolution and accepted it as fact. As a new Christian, I began to examine the evidence for evolution more closely and found it woefully inadequate to establish any fact. It takes more "faith" to believe that this exquisitely ordered creation came out of a random, meaningless event—that the intricacies of the human body evolved by a process of random mutations—that human intelligence came about by chance—than it does to believe that a supremely intelligent and loving God made it all. Why should I doubt God in favor of a man-made theory? All doubts about the Bible were laid to rest.[4]

After reading through the New Testament, I emphatically agreed with Psalm 119, which had spoken so clearly to me in the ashram: "I hate every false way!" I felt, and still feel, compassion and empathy toward all who are ensnared in false teaching, but I hate false ways because they keep people from knowing God's true love and grace. False teachers claim to reveal God's love, and I know from experience that a demon can make a person feel what seems like love. But the love of the true and living God is a saving, giving love—a love that made the way for us to know Him.

Grace was the power of God that had opened my eyes to see what a dark and horrific pit sin is, and how I could not save myself from it no matter how hard I tried. Grace is the love of God that knew, even before He created mankind, He would have to take on human flesh and die to save us from sin. Grace was God's giving *Himself* for me, even when I'd done nothing but reject Him and scoff at Him. Grace is the gift of God that cost Him dearly! Yet He gives it to us freely.

Yes, I hated false ways, and I was convinced that salvation could come by no means other than through faith in Jesus Christ. Although I didn't yet understand all that it meant to be "in Christ," I knew there had been no sin-bearer for mankind other than Jesus. No religious leader or teacher ever even claimed to die for the sins of mankind and be raised from the dead. In fact, all false teachers avoid the issue of sin in one way or another—by redefining it, minimizing it, or denying it altogether.

Jesus said, "I am the way, the truth, and the life; no one comes to the Father except through Me" (John 14:6). My former guru taught that Jesus didn't intend this claim personally, but rather that He referred to the "Christ-consciousness within Him." All false teachers distort or deny Jesus' claim to be the only way to God. They may try to hide their deception, as the guru did, by claiming association with Jesus, wearing cross pendants around their necks, or promoting moral principles. The fact that the guru did all these things was why I'd found it so hard to discern how something that seemed so good could be bad. When I finally realized that salvation is by grace alone, through faith in Jesus Christ alone, I saw that any teaching, no matter how good it seems, *is* bad if it keeps anyone from this truth: that faith in Jesus Christ is the only way to God.

False teachers of all sorts promise their followers great rewards from God, or even that they will be merged into God, but there is a common thread, one which appeals to human reasoning and pride: "You *can* earn your salvation, and you *must* earn it by doing something yourself." This is not grace. This is not truth. The only true and living God offers salvation—union and relationship with Him through His Spirit who dwells within believers—as a gift. Grace makes all the difference!

As a new follower of Jesus Christ, I couldn't help but be awestruck by grace. I had rejected God and His word over and over again, culminating in that critically decisive morning in April 1994, the morning I had consciously chosen not to bother finding a Bible to read about Jesus. I had chosen rather to meditate on syllables that didn't even make sense to me at the time. That morning I was not willing to seek the truth, but instead was easily satisfied with nonsense, not even able to recognize the danger I was approaching. My decision that day led not only to four more years of living in deception, but also to being sucked into a relationship with a demon whose sole purpose was to destroy me forever. Yet even when I was under the control of that demon, when at the ashram I faced the consequences of my decision, God reached out to me and sent me that which I'd rejected so many times: His word! God was my Rescuer, my Protector, my Savior even before I had acknowledged Him. He provided everything

I needed at the moment I needed it. Even when I was at the ashram, His Spirit began pouring out truth to me at the rate my heart could absorb. And now He had given me a new life—a life of meaning and purpose. It was more than I'd ever thought possible, beyond anything I could have hoped for during all those years of depression. What marvelous grace!

But as wonderful as all this was, I still had only a faint understanding of God's grace. I was forty years old by the time I was born again, when God took my old, dead spirit that had been separated from Him since my birth and replaced it with a new, living spirit, and put His Holy Spirit in me. My spirit was new, but my mind was still operating largely according to my old thoughts and ways. Life kept coming at me with the same speed and intensity, and as the months progressed I acted and reacted out of my old knowledge and understanding. Sometimes God's way won out over my ways, but many times it didn't. It took years for me to realize that my problem was unbelief—until I finally realized I needed to say, "Lord, I believe; help my unbelief!" (Mark 9:24).

"Help my unbelief!"

What does it mean to say, "Lord, I believe; help my unbelief"? Originally this plea came from a man asking Jesus to set his son free from a terrible demonic sickness. The distraught father asked Jesus, "If there is anything You can do, please help us." Jesus replied, "If you can believe, all things are possible for those who believe" (Mark 9:23). The man acknowledged that he did believe, but he was also straightforward enough to admit that he still had unbelief as well. Going into my new life, I believed with my whole heart and every fiber of my being that Jesus Christ is the only Savior, God in human flesh who died for my sins and rose again. If anyone had asked me if I believed the Bible was God's very word, I would have emphatically answered, "Yes!" and meant it. I wasn't even aware of the unbelief that was still in me.

The Heart-*Changer*

At the root of my problem was a lingering, gripping fear from having had such a close, personal relationship with a demon, the spirit behind the guru. This demon had been my constant, though invisible, companion. It had communicated with me through my thoughts and an inner voice. It had been, at first, the comfort I had longed for all my life (or so I thought). The demon spirit had been a counterfeit of the Holy Spirit. When I was born again the Holy Spirit came to live within me and wanted to be my comfort and strength, but I was afraid of mistaking the demon for the Holy Spirit again. To me, there was good reason to be cautious. After all, in the past the demon had quoted scripture to me. So, every time I thought I heard God or felt an urging by the Holy Spirit to do or say something, I hesitated: "Oh, is it really God, or is it *the demon*?" The bottom line is that I didn't trust that God was big enough and strong enough to shelter me from the demon. I desperately needed to know God better, but because of my fear, I couldn't! I loved a supernatural God, who is Spirit, but I was afraid of the supernatural and would not allow myself to be close to *any* spiritual being, even God.

I wasn't even able to express this fear for at least a couple of years. The closest analogy I ever found to describe it is this: Imagine a woman who, in her past, had been horribly molested, but now she has fallen in love with the man of her dreams, and they marry. When the time comes for her to give herself completely to her husband, she hesitates and shudders because of the memory of her abuse. How can such a woman participate fully in the marriage? She is unable because of fear. How could I participate fully in my relationship with God? I longed to be close to Him, but most times I hesitated out of fear and drew back.

Speaking again of the analogy, the only way such a marriage could survive and move forward would be for the loving husband to wait patiently for his wife to know him—to know that he is not like the one in her past who hurt her—and to shower his kindness on her so that she may know his love and no longer be afraid. This is exactly what God did for me. He patiently waited for me and gently guided me to a place and time at which I could receive His healing and believe Him.

But this took years because my fear was compounded by another problem: I believed my feelings more than God's word. For example, early in my new life, God led me to study the book of Ephesians, where I read wonderful things:

> Blessed be the God and Father of our Lord Jesus Christ who has blessed us with every spiritual blessing in the heavenly places in Christ, just as He chose us in Him before the foundation of the world, that we should be holy and without blame before Him in love, having predestined us to adoption as sons by Jesus Christ to Himself, according to the good pleasure of His will, to the praise of the glory of His grace, by which He made us accepted in the Beloved (Eph. 1:3-6).

How marvelous that God has blessed believers with every spiritual blessing! That He chose us before the foundation of the world! That He makes us holy and blameless before Him in love! That we are accepted in the Beloved!

How marvelous it would have been if I had believed all this applied to me! I believed that I had forgiveness of sins. I knew that God is holy and that Jesus died to take away the sin that so displeased God—that was so foreign to Him, that He couldn't even look upon. But to believe that God *accepted* me was much too contrary to all the rejection I had felt from early childhood on. I still didn't *feel* accepted because I still believed, thought, and felt according to my past. Without realizing it, I adopted a belief that God saved me because He had to. He created me, so He had little choice but to cleanse me, because He is God and therefore is moral and responsible. Yes, He would tolerate me, but to think that He actually loved and accepted me with any kind of affection was too much for me to believe. Not by coincidence, this was the core belief I had as a child about my parents.

My belief was contrary to God's word, but it had much power over me because it felt so true. Believing feelings above God's word is unbelief.

Worse yet, even though I believed that Jesus died for my sins, I felt as if the sins I committed as a Christian—not because I wanted to sin, or deliberately set out to sin, but usually because of selfishness and carelessness—broke my relationship with God. I heard other Christians talk about how sin cuts off fellowship with God. Quite often, I heard Christians begin their public prayers with "apologies" to God because we were not worthy or deserving to enter into His presence. They were correct, but incorrect at the same time. There is no doubt that none of us deserves to be in God's presence. The Bible tells us that it is only because of Jesus—because of His shed blood—that we have bold and confident access to God, but we who trust in Jesus do have it! Because of fear and unbelief, I didn't have a deep revelation of God's love, and I didn't yet know about all that Jesus' blood secured for me. To me, the underlying message from other Christians was that we were indeed saved by grace, but that after initial salvation it was our day-to-day performance that either sustained our relationship with God or cut it off. This wrong belief is called "legalism." It is also contrary to God's word; it is unbelief.

Even though God's gracious salvation had been "the event" of my life, and I had spent months rejoicing because of grace, my unbelief took me right back to focusing on my meager human efforts to deal with sin. Because I trusted my feelings over God's word, I fell for legalism, which in turn led me into a downward spiral—legalism fed into feelings of condemnation, which fed into more legalism, which fed into more condemnation. After all, how can a legalist ever know when she's done enough? She can only go by her feelings. When things felt right, that is, when I felt close to God, all seemed well. But when feelings of condemnation made God seem distant, I struggled to do "whatever it took" rather than simply believe God's word and trust Him. If I messed up, I felt condemned and tried harder in my own strength. I was no longer celebrating the grace of God!

Only a deeper relationship with God could take me beyond legalism, fear, and unbelief. I needed to spend as much time as possible with God, and I sensed that He was telling me to stop practicing law so that I could. I hesitated for months, second-guessing that it was a trick of the demon to get me to ruin my life again, or that it was my own desire—because I had wanted to stop practicing law for years. (It never occurred to me that God would actually allow me to do something I wanted to do!) After I was pretty sure that it really was God urging me to quit law, just to be safe, I sought out the advice of men in the church, who said, "No, you don't need to quit. The world needs Christian lawyers." Using my own reasoning, I could see that perhaps I could help people and serve God more as a Christian lawyer, and I had no idea what I'd do to support myself otherwise. So, I didn't quit. I disobeyed God. I believed my own reasoning and the opinions of men instead of God.

I'm not saying that every new Christian needs to give up his or her profession to start over with something new. I'm not even saying that every lawyer who becomes a Christian needs to give it up. I am saying that every Christian needs a lot time with God, and with my history I needed the spiritual equivalent of an intensive care unit! Because I didn't stop the busy pace that constantly competed for my time and attention, I delayed God's healing work in my life. I delayed the very changes I'd wanted all of my life. Eventually, God would see to it that I enter His intensive care, but the road there would have a few bumps—all caused by fear, unbelief, disobedience, and reliance on my own understanding.

Life Begets Life

Even though I came into my new life with these major problems, I did have new life! And life begets life. The truth that I knew and believed was that Jesus died for my sins and rose again from the dead to give me new life. So, I acted on this truth by telling others about forgiveness of sins through faith in Jesus. Evangelism became my way of serving God.

I spent as much time as I could with missionaries when they visited my church, and one such contact led to a ten day trip in March 1999 to Hungary, Slovakia, and Austria with a flute choir. We played in churches, concert halls, and schools, always focusing on the message of salvation from sin through Jesus Christ.

It was a childhood dream come true to perform on stages in Europe, but the highlight of the trip was seeing the power of God work in a woman in Budapest on a day when we combined sightseeing with evangelism. We used tracts to communicate the gospel since none of us knew more than a few pleasantries in their language. We left our bus that morning and set out on foot with plans of meeting it at another location in the afternoon. It turned out to be a national holiday in Hungary, and because of the parades and large crowds blocking the streets, meeting the bus became impossible. Long after the pre-arranged meeting time, our team was still separated from our bus and driver, with no way to call him. We took refuge from the cold in a coffee shop while our leaders tried to find the bus. For once, I listened to the Spirit of God and took the few remaining tracts outside to give to elderly people especially, because they had grown up under communism. I knew enough of the language to say, "Please take one," as I handed out the tracts, and I smiled and made eye contact with each person. So there would be no confusion, I approached only elderly women. Invariably, they would try to engage me in conversation. When I would say, in their language, "I'm sorry; I speak English," usually smiles and nods would follow as they moved on.

Chapter Five

I stood outside the coffee shop until dusk, and still our leaders were nowhere in sight. I had only two or three tracts left as the sun was setting. Two elderly ladies walked toward me, and I gave them each a tract. It was not uncommon in Hungary for people to stop immediately on the sidewalk to read a tract, and these ladies did so. One of them began to weep and hold out her hand to me. Even though she wasn't speaking English, somehow I knew she was saying, "Thank you, thank you! I have waited my whole life to know this! My whole life I have wanted this!" We both stood there, our hands held together. I couldn't answer her, but we communicated with our eyes. I understood the joy of meeting truth after a lifetime of yearning. I believe she received Jesus Christ as her Savior right there on the street. For her, one gospel tract in a language I couldn't even read made all the difference—all the difference in eternity.

The memory of my friends who remained at the ashram was always on my mind, and I prayed for them daily. They had religious zeal, but not in a way that would lead them to the truth. The thought of their being bound in deception and futility was more than I could stand. The only difference between them and me was that I had read the Bible while at the ashram. So, soon after returning from Europe, I formulated a plan to take Bibles to them. I wrote my former housemother to ask permission to visit my postulant sisters and, if possible, a few other nuns. When she said yes, the plan was underway for the July 4th weekend.

In preparation, I read the Bible from cover to cover for the first time in my life. Whole new vistas opened up to me, but the Holy Spirit especially impressed one theme on me, a theme that weaves all through the Scriptures: God is a heart-changer—the *only* Heart-Changer.

I first saw how God sees the human heart in Exodus and Deuteronomy. When Moses gave God's law to the people who had just come out of slavery in Egypt, they enthusiastically responded, "All God has said, we will do! We will be obedient!" (Ex. 24:7, author's paraphrase). But God knew their hearts. He said, "Oh, that they had such a heart in them that they would fear Me and always keep all My commandments, that it might be well with them and with their children forever!" (Deut. 5:29).

The people had no idea their hearts were so defective that they would not obey God no matter how much they promised. Centuries passed in which God's assessment was shown true. Generation after generation, the people disobeyed God and sinned in many ways, not the least of which was their continual worship of false gods. Through the prophet Jeremiah, God diagnosed their heart defect: "The heart is deceitful above all things, and desperately wicked" (Jer. 17:9). The human heart had long been infected by deceit—lies and falsehoods—so that the people were more willing to believe lies than God's truth. They were unwitting slaves to sin.

How would they ever be cured? How would they get a heart to believe God and obey Him?

God gave the answer through the prophet Ezekiel, who lived through very hard times. Because God's people had forsaken Him, He allowed their enemy to take them captive for seventy years. But even when Ezekiel was living as a captive in the enemy's land, God gave him messages of hope. Ezekiel relayed the good news of God's promise for their future—a time when He would change their hearts to love Him.

> "I will give you a new heart and put a new spirit within you; I will take the heart of stone out of your flesh and give you a heart of flesh. I will put My Spirit within you and cause you to walk in My statutes, and you will keep My judgments and do them" (Ezek. 36:26-27).

When and how is a human heart changed from being stony and rebellious to being soft and obedient toward God? This miracle begins when a person is born again—born of God. At the moment we receive Jesus Christ as Savior, God takes out the old rebellious heart that always wanted to stay far away from Him. He replaces it with a new heart and a new spirit that wants to obey Him. And His Holy Spirit comes to dwell in that new, clean heart. Formerly a slave of sin, the born again person is able to obey from the heart.

> But God be thanked that though you were slaves of sin, yet you obeyed from the heart that form of doctrine to which you were delivered (Rom. 6:17).

This discovery excited me. The time was drawing near when I would see my friends—with whom I had worshiped a false god—for the first time in two years. Would they see a difference in me? I was so far from what I wanted to be, but I had hope because God had changed my heart!

My companion for the trip was a Bible-study friend. We checked cartons of Bibles at the airport and, once in Los Angeles, gift-wrapped them along with treats allowed at the ashram. On the second day, with plenty of prayer support from my church back home and my friend in our hotel room, I loaded the boxes into the rental car and headed for the ashram. My goal was to proclaim the gospel, but not with argument or comparison. I wanted to show them how the truth had made a difference in my life, but I knew that God's Spirit would have to do the preaching.

First I met with the housemother, who, after evaluating my demeanor, permitted my former postulant sisters to come visit in groups of two or three at a time. As I sat alone in an enclosed garden waiting for the first group, one older nun slipped in quietly. Such a dear woman, she had been the picture of poise and kindness as she taught us about gardening. It was so good to see her. My heart was bursting to share the truth about Jesus with her, but if I did, there would be a chance I wouldn't get to see the others or leave the Bibles. We chatted for a few moments about her family, and she expressed her concern for some of them back home in Europe. She was hoping for changes in their lives. It wasn't the time or place to preach the gospel, but I shared a piece of the truth: "Only God can change a heart," I told her. She smiled her gentle smile and gazed deeply in my eyes, as if searching for the source of this wisdom.

She made her quiet exit as the postulants came. We shared updates about their lives and families, and some commented that I seemed contented and peaceful. Yes, I was more at peace than I'd ever been at the ashram, but still my heart was breaking for them. I wondered if my desire to be a witness to the truth of Jesus Christ was being accomplished. My doubt vanished on the arrival of a former roommate who stopped in her tracks and exclaimed, "Oh, Marcia, I wish I had a camera so I could take a picture of the way you are right now! You are different!" No change in my physical appearance inspired this response. Inwardly, I praised God for His Spirit living in me! And I prayed that she—that they all—would read the Bibles, to find the truth and love they were seeking.

I still don't know the impact the Bibles made, but thankfully I was able to see one result of the fervent prayers that weekend. Months later, one of my postulant sisters who had returned to Germany at the time of my visit, the one who had cooked the creative spaghetti dinner on my first night at the PA, came to live with me for three months. We took a trip to the Grand Canyon, and there, amid the splendor of God's creation, she received Jesus Christ as her Savior and Lord.

A New Mission Field

In the spring of 2001, I began training with a team from church for a two-week mission trip to Brazil in November. The closer it came to the actual trip, the more it seemed that God didn't want me to go. My desire to go faded with each passing week. During the same time, however, I had thoughts of going

Chapter Five

into jails and prisons to preach the gospel. The more frequently these thoughts came, the more my heart desired to do it.

Instead of going to Brazil, I went to a prison ministry training session and knew by the end of it that the Lord had called me to jails and prisons. His call was confirmed when the nauseating odor of the jail actually became sweet to me. And after a few months of hesitation, I acted on the Lord's instruction to leave my employer's law office to begin taking court-appointed assignments to defend indigent defendants. This became my ministry. Suddenly I no longer hated being an attorney! Now I lived and worked in my "mission field." I practiced law out of my home and spent as much time as possible in the jail visiting my clients. When we finished discussing their cases, and I was "off the clock," I listened to their concerns and problems. Many of them had never experienced anyone caring about them enough to listen. Being an effective advocate for them in court, and showing them I cared, opened opportunities to speak to them about Jesus. Each day I was gripped with the pressing need to tell the people I met—many of whose lives had been ravaged by drugs and alcohol—about Jesus.

The compelling urgency of it all was brought home to me especially in the case of one young man I'll call "Emilio." First arrested on drug charges, he spent a little time in jail. I was impressed with his considerate, soft-spoken manner. He knew he needed a change in his life, but like many young people in his position, he didn't understand the need to change immediately. He was more motivated by avoiding punishment than seeking real change. But his attitude soon did change because of a tragedy. After being released on bond, Emilio crashed his car into a cement guardrail. He survived the accident with a severe head injury, but his best friend was killed.

Emilio was charged in connection with the accident and re-arrested. As I was going to the jail to see him, I thought, "I'm not going to talk to Emilio about the Lord today, since his head must be throbbing so badly." When he came to the holding cell, I could see that he was in much pain. I said, "Oh, I'm so sorry, Emilio. Listen, I just want to tell you what to expect in court tomorrow, then I'll let you go lay your head back down." As I began to say a few words about the next day's preliminary hearing, Emilio interrupted me with a question: "Does Jesus really forgive sins?"

"Yes, He does. I wouldn't be here if He didn't."

"I need to be forgiven of so much."

"Emilio, have you ever considered receiving Jesus Christ as your Savior and Lord?"

"Yes. It's all I could think about last night, but I don't know how."

Emilio received Jesus as his Savior that day. The next day in court, it was quite noticeable that his pupils were unevenly dilated. I begged the judge for a conditional release so that Emilio could get immediate medical attention. The judge mercifully granted a recognizance bond.

Emilio did obtain treatment and over the next month recovered significantly. He called several times, and we had good discussions about Jesus and Emilio's desire to follow Him.

On the day of Emilio's next scheduled hearing, a felony arraignment, I thought it odd that I hadn't heard from him. We were scheduled for 2:00 p.m., and as I was leaving lunch, I called his relative's house to find him. A young woman answered the telephone, distraught and angry that I was asking to speak to Emilio. Another relative took the phone from her and told me that his body had been found earlier that morning in the middle of a road. He'd been murdered—shot in the head several times. It took a few hours for the reality of this devastating loss to sink in. As shock was replaced by mourning, there was comfort in the fact that, thirty days earlier, Emilio had trusted in Jesus and was now with Him.

The sense of urgency to preach the gospel to the people I was meeting every day intensified. I spent as much time in the jail as I could. One of the local judges eventually began to assign me probation revocation clients, which meant I could see more people. Opportunities to minister at a nearby maximum security prison arose as well.

I became more and more sure of my calling to jail and prison ministry. I never felt happier, safer, or more relaxed and fulfilled than when in a jail or prison teaching about Jesus Christ.

"Doing For" Instead of "Knowing Him More"

As a two-year-old Christian, I was happier than I'd ever thought possible. I had experienced more emotional healing in the few months after receiving Jesus than I previously thought possible in decades, largely because my life now had meaning and purpose—serving Him. Yes, I was doing a lot of *good* things for God. But I really needed to do the *best* thing—to know Him more. I had yet to learn that God wants obedience, not sacrifice. Although I hungered deeply for more of Him, I was still stunted in spiritual growth because of my fear and unbelief. My relationship with God was unstable, fluctuating as I struggled with feelings of condemnation.

When I asked at church about how I could know God better, the answer was always, "Read the Bible more." I was already reading the Bible several hours a day, but if I didn't believe God deeply loved and accepted me, how could I really believe the Bible—which from beginning to end is an explanation of all God has done to accept us because of His deep love?

I was spiritually paralyzed by unbelief. By observation and my own reasoning I concluded that the way to lead a victorious life was to devote myself to serving the Lord. The source of my satisfaction and security became doing what I thought God wanted me to do. Even though I'd been saved by grace, I wasn't living by grace. Instead, I was living by this formula: "The more I do for Him, the more likely it is that God will love and accept me; but because I don't feel loved and accepted, He hasn't really accepted me yet; therefore, I need to do more." I wasn't living by faith in the One who loved me enough to sacrifice Himself for me.

So, as I moved on with life, filling it with "service" and relying on my own reasoning, the next few years would be full of difficult circumstances created by my wrong decisions. God would use each one for His good purpose—to expose my fear and unbelief so that I would let Him deliver me and heal me. Even though I didn't know it going into this phase of my life, God's love for me was so great that He would patiently wait while I made mistake after mistake, even to the point of losing my ministry for Him. Through this process, I came to realize that He wasn't so much interested in what I could do for Him; He was very interested in giving more to me.

After the death of my stepfather in May 2002, I took a short trip to Gatlinburg for a change of scenery and visited a music shop full of handmade instruments. The owner and craftsman was a Christian who used his side building as a place for a new church to gather. He and his wife shared a contagious excitement about the new church, and I really wanted to go for the Wednesday night service. But I took one of their brochures and noticed that it mentioned speaking in tongues, laying on of hands, and something called the baptism of the Holy Spirit. These were things I'd heard about at my church only once or twice, and never in a good way. I thought, "Marcia, you've been tricked by a demon before, so you'd better not go." Instead of searching the word of God to see for myself if these things were true, I bowed down to fear. God was trying to guide me, but once again I didn't obey—out of fear. And I would live to regret this choice.

The day after returning home, I went to the jail to meet clients for upcoming probation revocation hearings. Just as I finished, the judge's secretary called to ask if I could take one more client for the next day. I went back to the jail, and they called the man out. The first time I saw him, there was a strong unsettled feeling in my gut, but I ignored it—true to my habit. He told me he'd been incarcerated in a neighboring state for seven months, and

Chapter Five

he'd devoted the time to reading the Bible, but that the jailers made him leave his Bible behind when they transferred him. He cried, "All I want to do is live for the Lord. I want to tell people they need Jesus. I want to get out of here and get back to that little church on Short Street, the one I went to as a kid." I was moved. Here was a man who seemed to have the same heart to tell others about Jesus, whose life God was redeeming from the pit, just as He had mine. Beyond that, I realized that the church this man was talking about was the church I attended. I told him we would certainly welcome him with open arms and gave him a Bible.

In court the next day, I argued that this man needed counseling, knowing that the judge would have no idea I was really referring to biblical counseling that was available at my church. The judge released him on the condition that he receive the counseling. He had no driver's license, so I picked him up for church and counseling sessions. He could be very charming.

Suddenly it seemed that the hunger I'd had for more of God was satisfied by my new relationship with this man, whom I'll call Fred. My old emotional habits intact, I allowed Fred to become dependent on me, and I felt responsible for his success or failure on probation. We spoke by telephone each day and spent time together walking on the high school track in the evenings. Some of the time we spent talking about God, and Fred seemed eager to know more. Much of the time, however, we spent talking about plans (not praying about them) for a jail and prison ministry together. I could see we were going to be a great team. A few weeks later we were married. Then he changed completely. The person he'd seemed to be was no longer evident. There was a demanding, even threatening, edge to his attitude toward me.

A few weeks after our marriage, I had a dream warning me that Fred would try to kill me. It was so disturbing that I awoke at 2:30 a.m., went to my computer, drafted a will, and took it to an all-night gas station to find attesting witnesses. But my old pattern had been to keep going no matter what, so after that night I put the dream out of my mind and put everything I had into

The Heart-*Changer*

the marriage. I catered to Fred, took care of him, and gave him practically everything he demanded—and he demanded quite a bit. My modest house wasn't enough for him, so I bought a bigger and better house, which I could barely afford. Even though he had no driver's license, Fred wanted a truck, then a bigger truck. It went on and on. Fred "couldn't" work because of back pain, which kept him on narcotic pain medication constantly. Even though he had no income, he never stopped demanding more, and sometimes he used threats of suicide to win his way. Mostly, he manipulated me through tapping into my feelings of condemnation—a weakness he exploited to his full advantage.

I was Fred's slave. When he knew I had a few moments to read the Bible, he would interrupt and insist that I get something for him. He stopped going to church and did everything he could to wreck my faith. I was trapped and miserable. Fred reneged on his promises to support my jail and prison ministry. In fact, he forbad me to continue. And because I had gone so far in debt to please him, I had to work longer and harder than ever just to stay afloat. There was no time to share the gospel with anyone. I had been rendered completely ineffective.

My marriage to Fred turned out to be yet another trick by which the evil one robbed me, this time not only of finances, but also of the ministry God had given me. My previous hunger to know God more had been easily derailed because of my fear of trusting Him completely. I feared intimacy with God, but fell into a deceptive intimate relationship with a fraud. I had taken another counterfeit. I had disobeyed God by failing to give up the practice of law and now had so much of it that it took all my time.

Many months of struggle passed, during which my precious moments in God's word were spent digging for answers that applied to me and my life. The time had come for the Bible to be a reality for me, not a collection of suggestions for some hypothetical life of some anonymous person out there. The Sermon on the Mount actually began to have significance in my life. By the grace of God, it came to the point where I could love

Fred the way Jesus tells us to love our enemies. When he was hungry, I fed him. When he cursed and menaced me, I showed no fear and prayed for his blessing.

But I still felt hopeless. I didn't sink to the level of depression I'd suffered earlier in life, but I did despair of ever finding a way out of this slavery. Many times I faltered, fighting with Fred in my own strength and my own words. Slowly I gained ground by refusing to fight him in this way. I jealously guarded my time alone with God, even if I had to lock myself in a room.

More than ever, God's word became my strength. Using verses from the book of Hosea, God began to show me that things would change. Even though I didn't understand everything entirely, in God's strength I gained courage to stand up to Fred's demands and refused to go further in debt.

At first, Fred didn't know how to react when I wouldn't be manipulated any longer, but within a month he left me and went to Florida, leaving behind long letters in which he threatened to harm me. Eventually he came back for more money, but he was arrested for violating a protection order I had obtained based on his threats. While in jail, Fred acted on information he knew to be false, telling others that I was hiding a quarter of a million dollars from him. For all intents and purposes, Fred put out a contract on me, offering to share this fictitious money with anyone who would help him kill me and dispose of my body. Soon after I learned of his plan, Fred was released from jail on bond. The danger seemed ominous to me.

Weeks went by under this threat, and Fred stalked me between court appearances. The uncertainty of it all seemed interminable. Even court officials, with whom I'd worked side by side, began to believe Fred's story that I'd stashed away a huge amount of money. I felt very much alone, but I relied on God's word:

> "No weapon formed against you shall prosper, and every tongue that rises against you in judgment you shall condemn. This is the heritage of the

servants of the Lord, and their righteousness is from Me," says the Lord (Is. 43:17).

Oh, how great is Your goodness, which You have laid up for those who fear You, which You have prepared for those who trust in You in the presence of the sons of men! You shall hide them in the secret place of Your presence from the plots of man; You shall keep them secretly in a pavilion from the strife of tongues (Ps. 31:19-20).

Though I walk in the midst of trouble, You will revive me; You will stretch out Your hand against the wrath of my enemies, and Your right hand will save me. The Lord will perfect that which concerns me; Your mercy, O Lord, endures forever; do not forsake the work of Your hands (Ps. 138:7-8).

I typed seven full pages of such encouraging verses and prayed them every day. I even kept them with me at counsel table in court.

Yet through this experience with Fred, I hit bottom. I had failed God in every way I'd ever tried to please Him. I came to realize that I had nothing—nothing whatsoever—to offer God. I came to know, experientially, what Jesus had said: "Without Me, you can do nothing" (John 15:5). But it was only when I hit bottom that I began to understand that God loved me because He wanted to, not because of anything I would do for Him. He showed me that *doing for* Him meant nothing in comparison to being in a loving relationship *with* Him. He lovingly let me know that He would restore me so that I could serve Him out of my love for Him rather than out of trying to gain His love—but that for the time being I just needed to know Him, rest in Him, and learn to trust Him. My hunger to know God more revived, and

Chapter Five

I was absolutely sure that I *could* know Him more—more of His power, love, strength and wisdom. I began attending a different church, one with a statement of faith that included speaking in tongues, laying on of hands, and the baptism of the Holy Spirit.

It may not have been the best thing to do, but because of Fred's threats, I bought a revolver and shotgun in early June 2004 and took a class on how to shoot them. When I practiced with the shotgun, the force of the "kick" against my shoulder exacerbated the weakness in my neck that had remained from the car accident many years before. The shotgun blasts actually forced my neck vertebrae out of place, so that the pressure on the nerves was practically unbearable. On the way home from class, I bought a neck brace because I couldn't hold my head up. Then, at home, all I could do was recline and listen to the Christian channel on television. I seldom turned it on, but that day I heard teaching that was quite timely. It was a program featuring a man with an international healing ministry, mostly centered in Africa. He spoke about Isaiah 53:5, that "by Jesus' stripes we are healed." He told of the many miraculous physical healings he'd seen.

"Wow," I thought, "I wonder if that's really true." In my former church, I'd been taught that this verse referred to spiritual healing only—the forgiveness of sins.

The next morning I drove to my new church. It was only the third week of my attendance there, and I didn't want to draw attention to myself, so I took off the neck brace before going in. But during Sunday school class, the pain became intense, and my head became so heavy that I had to put the neck brace on for the church service. In a time of prayer, a woman behind me noticed the brace and laid hands on it. I listened closely to her prayer, and when she said, "For we know, Lord, that by Your stripes she is healed," I thought, "It *IS* true!" Immediately the vertebrae moved back into place. I tore off the brace, and the pain vanished.

The next Sunday, the pastor invited anyone seeking the baptism of the Holy Spirit to come to the altar. While I was there, he put his hand on my head and prayed for me. Just as he took his hand away, a holy power came on me—the power of the Holy Spirit. Jesus' presence was there, and I was at His feet, my heart overflowing with praise and thanksgiving. Just as the night of March 22, 1998, the praise was so intense that it could not be expressed in language I knew, but the Holy Spirit gave me a new language to use. I spoke in tongues as the Spirit gave me utterance and had deep communion with Jesus.

As I came to know more of God's love, His Spirit opened up the Scriptures more and more. Slowly I began to rely on Him more. My relationship with Him was beginning to be the source of satisfaction in my life.

Fred and I were divorced, and he actually served eight months in prison for his antics. After his release, he tried one more time to get money from me, but it didn't work. For one thing, I had none to give. I was working hard just to pay the debts created by his demands and medical expenses. Within a short time, Fred incurred a DUI charge and fled to a distant state to avoid arrest on the warrant. He later died there of a heart attack.

Learning to Trust and Obey

By the spring of 2005, I was facing imminent and drastic changes in my lifestyle because of an impending financial collapse due to the large debt I was carrying. In early April, God showed me a simple but effective plan to get out of debt. I would have to sell my houses and live with my mother with as few expenses as possible. My earnings were to go toward paying back the debt.

The very next morning after I'd received this plan, I happened to have a chance meeting with a man I hadn't seen since high school, whom I'll call Leonard. He asked me to dinner, but I turned him down. He was separated from his wife and children and in the process of divorce. But honestly, it wasn't so much his life circumstances that led me to turn him down. He was Catholic, and there was no way I wanted near anyone or anything that would bring up my past days as a Catholic. Inwardly, I was

Chapter Five

still hiding from that shame. But over the course of a few weeks, Leonard was persistent, and he seemed to be a caring person. He began showing up at my church. I thought, "Maybe I should give him a chance."

By now it should be fairly predictable that my old emotional habits and patterns led to a new set of problems. Actually, it was the same old set of problems with a different name and face. Yes, this man "needed" me. He was hurting from his prior marriage, and he needed a lot of support.

Moreover, in my own reasoning and understanding, I thought his children also needed me. On a Sunday morning a few weeks prior to the chance meeting with Leonard, my pastor had said something to the effect that ministry to young people was more effective than jail or prison ministry because God can change a young person's life before they make the choices that lead to incarceration. This statement came as a bit of a shock. Even though I hadn't yet returned to jail or prison ministry, in my heart I still felt called to it. I asked, "Lord, is that true? Is youth ministry better than jail and prison ministry?" God didn't answer my question directly, but simply said, "I will give you a ministry with children." I responded with a skeptical chuckle of unbelief, "Well, You're really going to have to change me for *that*!" After a few weeks of dating Leonard, my own reasoning went full steam ahead to the conclusion that his children "must be" the ones God had meant for my ministry. Further, as Leonard and I considered a future together, we wanted to adopt a daughter from China. "In faith," we even named her. Oh, it all seemed to fit together so perfectly! *I* could see that an adopted daughter would not only be a ministry, but also it surely would be the mechanism by which the Lord would heal my past. It all seemed so right—to me.

So, I rushed into yet another marriage. And again, within a few months, everything changed. My husband's trust was replaced by suspicion; his goodwill, by condemnation. My long hours at the law office, still necessary because of my debt, led Leonard to believe that I was being unfaithful. He continually brought up

The Heart-Changer

my past, especially as it related to my illicit affair eighteen years earlier. A spirit of condemnation loomed over me constantly. Too often, I tried to defend myself from Leonard's accusations. I tried to reason with him, but the situation only grew worse. I was by no means faultless. Most of my "reasoning" led only to nastier arguments and hurtful words said in spite. The strife gave rise to a brooding cloud of confusion and evil in our home. I resented Leonard's accusations and gradually became bitter and unforgiving toward him.

Each Saturday morning, with Leonard at work, I had a few hours to myself, and I used the time to be with God, in His word. These weren't moments full of gloriously good emotions. I was desperate. It was a struggle to come to God because I felt so guilty over my situation, but I couldn't survive if I stayed away from Him. As I brought my issues and struggles into these moments, many times all I could do was cry. But God didn't abandon me when times were tough.

On one such Saturday morning in late February 2006, as I was praying about my finances, God led me to the fourth chapter of Second Kings, where a prophet told a widow how to get out of debt. All she had was a little cruse of oil. The prophet told her to borrow as many pots as she could and just keep pouring. Miraculously, her little jar of oil filled all the pots. She sold the oil, paid her debts, and had enough to live on. As I pondered this passage, I prayed, "But what do I have that is like the widow's oil?" The answer was the Holy Spirit. Instead of working more, I was to get back to jail and prison ministry and pour this oil into as many "pots" as possible. God confirmed this instruction again and again through other Bible passages and sermons.

Before I could get back into a prison to minister, Leonard filed for divorce in March. I put everything I had into seeking reconciliation, and we did resume our marriage in late April. However, literally days after we were back under the same roof, the accusations and condemnation started all over again, worse than ever.

Chapter Five

Yet in all the turmoil, God's direction was consistent. One afternoon, in a moment of reflection and prayer, I considered how out of control my life was. Even with my monstrous debt and my marriage in shambles, God brought my attention back to His instruction in 1999 that I'd never obeyed—to leave the practice of law. I thought of all the arguing involved in the practice of law and said, "Father, I really don't think You want me in this profession. I mean, it just seems to feed the strife and contention that are already too strong in my personality. Just tell me what You want me to do, and I'll do it."

Immediately, He said in the still, small inner voice, "Why don't you step out on faith, and I'll take care of your debt." I got up to find the newspaper to search the help wanted ads. The only job for which I was arguably qualified was a salesperson, but I didn't apply because I'd failed miserably in sales jobs as a college student. Soon after, a job became available that conformed to God's wishes, one in which I was still marginally in law, but with little or no strife. The new position would require much less time than my private law practice, but my income would be drastically reduced. I wrapped up my practice and began my new job in July.

Also in July, I learned of an opportunity to minister at the prison in August. I wouldn't play much of a role in the program, but would be there for support. It turned out to be a watershed event in my relationship with God.

On August 13, 2006, I was sitting in a seat just in front of the inmates in the large chapel of the maximum security prison, facing the platform. A wonderful woman of God was telling the story of her life. Her father had abandoned her family many times and had spent much of his life behind bars. She had prayed for him constantly, even telling God that she would give her own life, if necessary, for her father to be saved. She finished by telling us how her father had been released from prison for the last time at an old age and how he had received Jesus Christ before he died.

The Heart-*Changer*

Her story bore no similarity to mine, but it was powerful to me. As she spoke, the Holy Spirit moved mightily on me as I realized I had never given myself completely to God as this woman had, nor trusted Him the way she did. In just a few seconds, the Holy Spirit showed me how I had relied on my own reasoning and resorted to self-will instead of trusting God and obeying His word. The power of His grace prevailed in my heart that day. I realized that in 1998 I had received Jesus, but I had not fully surrendered myself to Him. Right there in the prison chapel, in the midst of the inmates, I silently confessed, "Lord, I know I should have done this eight years ago, and You deserved it then. I didn't even know I was holding back, but I was. I come to You now, and I give my whole self to You. I'm not holding anything back. I surrender everything to You. I don't want to take even one step without You." His love and cleansing poured out in my heart like a flood. There I was, in the middle of a maximum security prison, being set free in the presence of God!

I went home a new woman. God showed me from the life and psalms of David that I didn't have to defend myself, because He will defend and protect me. God is mighty, so all we have to do is return good for evil and walk in His love. I forgave Leonard. Even so, he left me for the last time in late August. There was no argument, no "scene" from me. I stood in the grace of God. I was calm and kind. I knew God would be my Defender.

Yet, after Leonard left and filed for divorce again, the feelings of condemnation were overwhelming. This marriage and divorce were brought on by my own immature understanding and my sin of prideful self-will. I could see it clearly, but seeing it didn't make it all go away. Two divorces within a matter of three years! Such failure! How could I ever minister to anyone in the name of Jesus again? I was finished, or so it seemed. The more I gave into the feelings of condemnation and hopelessness, the more I doubted that I'd ever be able to trust that I was hearing God correctly—and the old, nagging fear of the demon crept back to the forefront of my life.

Chapter Five

I was nearing another crossroads. In the eight years since I'd become a Christian, my own fear, unbelief, and self-will had limited God, but in all my struggles, He had been faithful to me. He never abandoned me. Just the opposite, He was always there to pick me up when I fell to a new low. His grace kept me going. As I had taken each baby step of trust and surrender, God had shown Himself strong. When I finally surrendered all to Him, He began to heal and change me deeply—as He had wanted to all along. He no doubt would have preferred that I'd believed and surrendered fully from the very start, but failing that, He was ready to use my fear, failure, and weaknesses to show me His power and love. A new chapter of my life—the best chapter—was ready to begin.

Chapter Six

~ ~ ~

Intensive Care

The next few months were an opportunity to learn how to trust God completely to provide for every need. Pending the divorce proceedings, it was my responsibility to maintain the homes and pay the mortgages on two properties; and this responsibility came after I'd already reduced my income by about seventy-five percent. But God had promised He would take care of my debt. Even though it looked as if there was no way it could be done, God did it. Much of the time, I marveled at how He did it, but He always enabled me to make every payment for every bill and debt on time.

There were times, however, when I wondered if those properties would ever sell. The economy was getting worse, and it was a buyer's market. A few prospective buyers had looked at one house, but none at the other. One cold winter day, as I was getting in my car to leave from checking the house that had sparked no interest from anyone, I heard the Lord tell me to lay hands on the house. I got out of the car, put my hands on the house, and prayed: "In the name of Jesus, I declare this house is sold—sold at a fair price—and that it will be a blessing to the family who buys it." Within twenty-four hours, the realtor called with a firm offer of a fair price from a family who said the house was just what they needed. Later that month, the sale of both houses closed on the same day.

Finally, in March 2007, I did what God had told me to do in 1999. At last I entered the "spiritual intensive care unit" I had

The Heart-Changer

needed for many years. I started spending most of the day, every day, with God, in His word. The more time I spent with Him, the more I wanted—and the more healing came to my heart and mind. He lovingly began to expose my heart, peeling back layer by layer and healing each one as He went. I didn't seek out special passages of Scripture to deal with my specific problems; I studied the Bible just to know God more. He is ever so willing to reveal Himself. As I read about His relationship with the people in the Bible—Adam and Eve, Cain and Abel, Abraham and Sarah, Joseph and his brothers, Moses and the people of Israel, David and the other kings—the Holy Spirit showed me more and more of who God is: His nature, character, attributes, and personality. Simultaneously, I learned about myself.

I'm not sure if it is this way with everyone, but in my case, the outer layers of the heart God peeled back first dealt with the most recent pain, from the most recent lies I'd believed. Having just gone through my second divorce in three years, I was devastated to think I had ruined any purpose God may have had for my life, and I struggled with feelings of condemnation. I lapsed back into the mind-set that God's acceptance depended on me, and that my mistakes had disqualified me for it. But God revealed His ways in the life of Abraham.

God told Abraham to move from his homeland to a land he didn't know, and He promised He'd give it to Abraham and his descendants forever. But Abraham was already seventy-five years old, and his wife sixty-five, and they had no children. Even though God's promise looked impossible to the human eye, Abraham believed, and God counted his faith as righteousness.

So, how did reading about this infertile elderly couple who lived thousands of years ago give me hope? I saw how God responded to Abraham's mistakes.

Abraham obeyed God and came from his homeland into Canaan, but he soon encountered a famine so severe that he had to go to Egypt. Abraham turned to Sarah and said, "You are a beautiful woman, and when the Egyptians see you they will want you. They will kill me to have you. Please tell them you're my sister, and we'll both survive" (Gen. 12:11-13, author's paraphrase). It all happened just as Abraham predicted. Pharaoh, the king of Egypt, saw Sarah's beauty and took her into his harem. He treated Abraham very well for her sake. But God caused Pharaoh and his household to have major problems because he had taken Abraham's wife. When Pharaoh found out the truth, he sent Abraham and Sarah on their way.

Abraham hadn't trusted God enough, so he thought he had to protect himself by resorting to his own reasoning and tactics. But this incident happened early in Abraham's walk with God, so perhaps it's understandable that he didn't know God well enough to trust Him. Well, twenty-five years later, Abraham did the same thing!

When Abraham was ninety-nine years old, God told him that his son, the miracle son of promise, would be born the next year. The elderly couple traveled to a place called Gerar. Once again, Abraham told the king, Abimelech, that Sarah was his sister. And once again, the king took Sarah for himself—although God kept him from touching her. God came to Abimelech in a dream and told him he was a dead man unless he restored Abraham's wife. When Abimelech asked Abraham why he would do such a thing, Abraham replied, "It's the same thing I did before, right after God first brought me out of my homeland. I said she was my sister so people in a foreign land would not kill me to have her" (Gen. 20:13, author's paraphrase).

Abraham admitted that he was still thinking and behaving the same way he had twenty-five years earlier! Through the years he had come to know God better and better, but in this one area he had not let God change his thinking.

The Holy Spirit showed me that I had done the very same thing in the two marriages. I had acted on old ways of thinking that had been established in my mind and heart long before I'd even known the Lord, let alone started to trust Him with my whole life. I had acted on the need to be needed, because I thought I'd surely be rejected if the other person wasn't dependent on me. I was still living by my own understanding instead of trusting God.

But I was so encouraged! It had been just after God promised Abraham that his son would soon be born that he had risked it all by giving his wife to Abimelech. Yet God protected and preserved Sarah so that she could bear the son of promise, Isaac. In other words, God fulfilled His promise to Abraham in spite of his mistake! This gave me great hope! I thought, "Since God doesn't make a difference between people, and He'll do for one what He's done for others, my life is not wasted by my mistakes! The best years are yet to come!"

Believing this promise, I continued in God's intensive care, and He continued to heal me through His word and His Spirit in the progressively deeper layers of my heart.

Deeper and Deeper Healing

Each year since 1986, the time from April 18 (the anniversary of Steve's heart attack) and May 6 (the anniversary of his death) had always been difficult, and 2007 was no exception. But in God's intensive care, it turned into a great blessing.

Around April 18, God began to explain the effects of emotional pressure from the death of a loved one, using an incident in the life of Moses found in Numbers chapter twenty. Moses had just lost his sister, Miriam. He'd been through a lot with her, and her death was no doubt painful to him. Adding to this emotional pressure, the people of Israel complained against him and against God because they had no water. They forgot about all the times God had miraculously provided them with food and water. In fact, forty years earlier, their parents had drunk water that God caused to pour from a rock when Moses struck it with his walking stick. Now they were in a similar situation, but they failed to remember God's goodness and chose to complain.

Chapter Six

They had grumbled many times before, and Moses had handled it perfectly by the grace of God. He had humbled himself by falling on his face before God. His attention had been on God rather than on himself, and he hadn't cared how he looked in front of his critics. This time, the pain from Miriam's death was added pressure on him, and in this emotional state he put his focus on himself. Upset at the grumblers, he stomped away from them to the door of the tabernacle—the special tent where God's presence dwelled. There, he fell on his face and heard God's very specific instructions.

He was to take the walking stick—the same one he'd used on the rock forty years earlier—and gather the people before the rock. This time, Moses was only to speak to the rock, and God would cause water to flow.

But Moses was still upset. He took the rod and gathered the people as commanded, but instead of just speaking to the rock, he struck it twice—and he spoke sharp words to the people.

Moses' emotions had led him to disobey God's instructions. God called it unbelief. He said, "Because you did not believe in Me, to show me to be holy in the eyes of the people, you shall not bring them into the Promised Land" (Num. 20:12, author's paraphrase). The incident lived on in infamy, being referred to as the "water of strife" (Ps. 106:32). Because of Moses' unbelief in this strife-filled incident, he wasn't allowed to enter the Promised Land.

God used this incident to show me that the emotional pain associated with Steve's death, which had long been lodged in my heart, had to go. Because of it, I was always more likely to enter into strife when under pressure. It was a vulnerability the evil one had used and could continue to use against me, to rob me of my "promised land"—love, joy, and peace in the Holy Spirit.

I heard this message from God on April 20, and I wish I could report that I heeded His warning. But no, I permitted myself to entertain the old thoughts and feelings about the circumstances of Steve's death twenty-one years before—resulting in the same

The Heart-*Changer*

guilt, regret, and self-pity. By May 6, I was so caught up in my own drama of self-focus that I ignored the needs of my mother in whose house I was living. On that day, the anniversary of Steve's death, a situation arose which brought up the same feelings of rejection and shame I'd endured since childhood. Under this "emotional pressure," I responded with strife-filled words.

It had happened again! I had failed again! When I retreated to solitude, I heard the gentle voice of the Lord say, "Do you want to remain a child all your life?" Immediately, by the power of His Spirit, I saw what He meant: How long would I hold on to the hurt and self-pity? Didn't I want to grow up and mature in Him? Yes, I did! I told Him so, and He replied, "Then give this to Me." Giving it to Him meant making a conscious choice to let go of my control, to be willing to face the pain and guilt, and to trust Him with my deep feelings. For decades, I'd been too afraid to do it. But within twenty minutes of giving it over into His hands, much of the hurt that I'd carried for so many years was gone—healed.

I remained in His presence as He revealed to me, in great love and without condemnation, how holding onto the hurt and self-pity had affected my life and the lives of others. Going even deeper, He also showed me that my resentment toward Him had been the underlying cause of all the self-pity I'd carried all those years. He showed me as much as I could understand at the time. I confessed my resentment, and it evaporated in His forgiveness. I also acknowledged all the damage and hurt I had caused. I received His forgiveness for all of it, and He healed this layer of my heart.

But I wanted more. I wanted to be completely free of the stranglehold my past seemed to have on me. I prayed, "Father, please root this out of me once and for all, down to the core. Show me *the* answer from Your word, in the name of Jesus, and thank You in advance."

Chapter Six

Still Deeper

In God's intensive care, He uses everything for His purpose. For example, in July 2007 I ran out of money and prayed for another job. Within a few days, I saw an ad in the newspaper for medical office cleaners. I was glad to get the job and worked about ten hours per week in the evenings for $7.00 per hour. The pay didn't trouble me, because somehow God always managed to cover all my needs. The nature of the work wasn't a problem; I actually enjoyed cleaning. What bothered me tremendously was the fact that, as a cleaning lady, I was invisible to the medical staff. They acted as if I didn't even exist. My pride couldn't handle not being noticed, so I'd position myself within earshot of the doctors and nurses and carry on conversations with my co-worker in which I'd make sure I sounded very, very intelligent. "It's important that they know I'm not *just* a cleaning lady," I thought. After all, *my dignity* was at stake!

God had a work to do in my heart—to get to the pride—and this job was a tool in His hands, like a sculptor's chisel. And if the cleaning job was the chisel, then His Word was the hammer which gave it force to remove the pride and arrogance that weren't fitting for a child of God. Over the two and one-half years that I would hold this job, God would lovingly chisel away until I was content being unseen and unappreciated by others—a change made possible only when I truly knew He cared for me, and this knowledge could only come through His word and His Spirit.

In the men and women of the Bible, God exposed my own heart. And in May 2008, He revealed *the* answer for which I'd prayed a year earlier. In order to understand myself, I had to go back to the beginning, to the first three chapters of Genesis.

Nearly everyone has heard of Adam and Eve, the first humans, but not everyone has heard the details of their lives in the Garden of Eden.[5] They had everything they could've ever wanted: abundant food, beautiful surroundings, satisfying work, and, most of all, love. They had a completely unhindered, loving relationship with God. They knew Him as their Creator and Friend. Plus, the relationship between Adam and Eve was ideal. They were so focused on God and each other that they could be naked yet not ashamed. They lived and breathed in an atmosphere of love. It was all "very good"—even God said so (Gen. 1:31).

But God wanted more for Adam and Eve. He wanted them to be perfect. He had created them in His own image with free will, so they had the power to choose whether they would love Him or not. Their obedience would show their love. If they would choose to obey Him, they would be perfectly lined up with the perfect will of God. So, He had to give them an opportunity to choose. He gave them one restriction: "You may eat freely from every tree of the garden except the tree of the knowledge of good and evil. You shall *not* eat of it. The day you do, you will surely die" (Gen. 2:16-17, author's paraphrase).

With all their needs met, Adam and Eve would have had little reason to think of the forbidden tree—until the tempter came along.

The tempter was none other than Satan himself, the evil one. God had created him as Lucifer, a beautiful angel, to worship God at His throne, but Lucifer had rebelled and actually wanted to take God's place (Isa. 14:12-15). God had cast him out of heaven, along with multitudes of other rebellious angels, now called demons (Rev. 12:9). In the garden, Lucifer, now Satan, pursued his agenda—to attack God through His most beloved creatures, Adam and Eve. If Satan could get them to disobey, they would become his slaves and work against God's will.

Satan began his attack with a sly question to Eve about God's word: "Did God really say you can't eat of every tree of the garden?" Suddenly, Eve's focus was on the one thing she couldn't have, and she felt a lack for the very first time—exactly the effect Satan wanted. He knew that Eve would want to satisfy the feeling of lack, and his goal was to deceive her into satisfying it herself rather than relying on God. Satan knew he was no match for God, but the woman without God would be easy prey. If Eve would

Chapter Six

have called out to God for help with this new, uncomfortable feeling, He would have come, answered the question, and put an end to her feeling of lack.

But she didn't. She focused on the lack. Eve took her focus off God and put it on her circumstances. Then she tried to fend for herself. She answered the serpent, "We may eat the fruit of the trees in the garden, but not the tree in the middle of the garden. God told us, 'You shall not eat of it, nor shall you touch it, lest you die'" (Gen. 3:2-3, author's paraphrase). Eve changed God's word. She added a restriction that wasn't from God at all. God didn't say they couldn't touch the tree. When Eve changed God's word, she became more susceptible to believing a lie when the tempter flatly contradicted it: "You won't die! God only said that because He knows when you eat of the tree, your eyes will be opened and you'll be like Him, knowing good and evil" (Gen. 3:4-5, author's paraphrase).

Satan not only contradicted God's word; he also challenged His very character. The evil one essentially said that God had lied and was withholding something good from Adam and Eve. Did Eve respond by saying, "No way, serpent! God would never do anything like that because He loves us"? How about, "No, I don't believe you, serpent, because God would never lie"? Did she even call out to God to help her in this tense moment? No. What did she do? She "saw for herself."

The Bible says that throughout the six days of creation, God had looked at what He had made and called it good. After He created Adam and Eve, He said it was very good—and His evaluation was all that mattered. But now Eve was thinking for herself. Instead of relying on God's evaluation of things, she saw for herself that the forbidden fruit was good for food, pleasant to her eyes, and desirable to make her wise.

Eve felt a lack and wanted to satisfy it, but she didn't call out to God. With the serpent's lie still in her ears, Eve doubted God's goodness, so how could she trust Him to satisfy her lack? She didn't. She trusted herself to get what she felt she needed. She had believed the lie—actually a double lie: that God wasn't good and that there were no consequences for disobeying Him. Then she acted independently of God. She plucked the fruit and ate it.

What a quick descent into disobedience! Eve went from feeling a lack, to fending for herself, to changing God's word, to distrusting God, to believing a lie, to acting independently of God in one brief moment! Even more amazing is that Adam, who was with her, wasn't even deceived by the serpent. He simply decided to eat the fruit! Adam deliberately acted independently of God—and acting independently of God is sin.

As God showed me this pattern—how the feeling of lack leads to acting independently of Him—His Spirit also helped me see how I had fallen into it repeatedly, countless times in all kinds of situations. He also helped me understand that the unhealed emotional wounds from my past made me constantly vulnerable to the feeling of lack in the present. They were "triggers." The picture He gave me was that my heart was like a deep well, and the wounds from the past were like the water near the bottom. If all was calm on the surface, then the deep water was also untroubled. But if anything disturbed the surface, even the deep water was agitated. My unhealed emotional wounds didn't cause so much of a problem when everything was all right, but if there was added stress or pressure, then I felt threatened to the core—a strong feeling of lack. By permitting these wounds to remain in my heart, I was allowing myself to be constantly vulnerable to the feeling of lack and the strategy of Satan.

Lack doesn't always come in the form of wanting something we can't have. It comes any time we feel that our happiness, our position in life, or our dignity is threatened. Whenever we feel that we'll be diminished in any way, we feel lack. And lack is the emotional response Satan needs to take us down the path of sin. Once we feel lack, we are tempted to put our focus on our circumstances and our own ability to satisfy it instead of keeping our focus on God. When we act independently of God to take care of ourselves instead of trusting Him to do it, we sin—exactly what Satan wants us to do.

The evil one's strategy is to get us wrapped up in the feeling of lack and the desire to fill it. But we *can't* feel lack if we know God's goodness and trust Him fully—if we keep our focus on Him! If we remember who God truly is and how He loves us, we won't have the emotional response of lack, at least not for long. So, Satan disguises his strategy in different circumstances, so we are tempted to think, "*This* time it's different. *This* time I'm justified in trusting myself rather than God. *This* time I have to take care of myself." The circumstances may be different, but the temptation is the same. We are never justified in distrusting God or acting independently of Him.

What happens when we do? What happens when we've acted independently of God because we've tried to satisfy our lack? Again, to understand ourselves, we have to look at Adam and Eve.

As soon as they ate the forbidden fruit, they knew they were naked. Suddenly their attention was on themselves, and the strong bond of love was broken. They felt self-conscious and ashamed. But they still didn't cry out to God for help. Instead, they tried to take care of the situation by making leaf aprons to cover themselves.

Next they hid from God in the shadows of the trees. Previously they had known and trusted God as their Friend, but their sin was an act of unloving rebellion against Him, and now they tried to hide from Him out of fear. They chose the darkness over God's light.

But God's love for Adam and Eve had not changed. He gave them an opportunity to come back to Him, to confess their sin. God asked Adam, "Did you eat of the tree against My command?" (Gen. 3:9-11, author's paraphrase). This was their big chance to throw themselves on God's mercy.

But Adam and Eve had changed. Sin had penetrated and infected their hearts.

Adam no longer trusted God or loved Eve as he had before. He just wanted to defend himself, and he was willing to shift the blame to do it. So, instead of confessing his sin to God, Adam blamed Eve *and* God for his own wrongdoing: "The woman *You* gave me did this. She ate from the tree, gave me some of the fruit, and I ate it, too" (Gen. 3:12, author's paraphrase).

Eve was also unwilling to admit her fault. When God asked her what she'd done, she didn't admit that she had distrusted Him and disobeyed His word. She didn't ask for mercy. She blamed the serpent for deceiving her.

Again, I could see how this pattern had played over and over again in my past. When I felt pressured or threatened, I had reacted to lack and defended myself with anger, strife, and bitterness. Then I felt guilty and ashamed, but I didn't run to God. No, I hid from Him and tried to cover up my feelings with all kinds of things—self-pity, ambition, relationships, food, work, drugs, and religion (to name a few). Worse yet, I had spent my life blaming God and other people for my own sin.

Did Adam and Eve die that day, as God said they would? Yes, they did, but not physically. When they distrusted and disobeyed God, their spirits became separated from His. They were physically alive, but spiritually dead. Every human being has inherited this spiritual death from Adam and Eve. We are all born with sin-infected hearts and spirits that are separated from God (Rom. 5:12-21). This is why we all need to be born again.

The great news is that right there in the Garden of Eden, God promised that someday Someone would come to heal sin-infected hearts and make things right again (Gen. 3:15). This Someone is Jesus, God in human flesh. Jesus lived only to do God's will. From the day of His birth, to the day of His death on the cross, to His resurrection and ascension into heaven, Jesus acted only in God's perfect will. "Though He was a Son, yet He learned obedience by the things He suffered. And having been perfected, He became the author of eternal salvation to all who obey Him" (Heb. 5:8-9). Jesus was perfected by doing what Adam did not do—obey God perfectly. And when we place our faith in Him, His righteousness is credited to us, as if we had obeyed God perfectly. And we are born again—with new hearts that desire to obey God, new spirits that are alive to Him, and the Holy Spirit within us to enable us to obey. What a merciful, gracious God! Jesus is the ultimate answer. With this revelation from Genesis, I had a new, deeper appreciation for all He had done for me.

God had shown me *the* answer I had prayed for—how in everyday life this sinful habit of reacting to the feeling of lack can be stopped. The answer is to know God and trust that He will always take care of any lack, so we don't have to fend for ourselves. We must call out to God as soon as we feel anything other than joy and peace in Him. God wants us to bring everything to Him!

> "God resists the proud, but gives grace to the humble." Therefore humble yourselves under the mighty hand of God, that He may exalt you in due time, casting all your care upon Him, for He cares for you. Be sober, be vigilant; because your adversary the devil walks about like a roaring lion seeking whom he may devour. Resist him, steadfast in the faith (1 Pet. 5:5-9).

In these verses, God explains that He will always give us grace to handle our circumstances when we humbly obey Him, depend on Him to defend and provide for us, and wait for His timing. To prevent the feeling of lack, we must throw all our care upon Him—all worries, concerns, problems, and negative emotions. We weren't meant to carry these ourselves, and when we try to handle them we end up feeling lack. God cares for us, so it is safe to cast all our care on Him. Any time we feel anything other than joy, peace, and security in God, we need to run to Him immediately and give Him our feelings. In prayer, we must put them in His hands and let go. This is the way we resist the devil! If we don't linger in the feeling of lack, we won't give in to temptation.

When the deceiver comes disguised in any circumstance, we must remember that it's really not about "the tree"! It's not about the circumstances. It's about whether we trust God to be who He says He is.

But what if we blow it—if in the heat of emotion we react to lack and act independently of God? What can we do? No matter what, we must come out of the shadows and run to God—the sooner the better!

> He who covers his sins will not prosper, but whoever confesses and forsakes them will have mercy (Prov. 28:13).

> If we confess our sins, He is faithful and just to forgive us our sins and to cleanse us from all unrighteousness (1 John 1:9).

> But if we walk in the light as He is in the light, we have fellowship with one another, and the blood of Jesus Christ His Son cleanses us from all sin (1 John 1:7).

When our hearts feel guilty, we don't want to run to God. We want to hide. Jesus' blood cleanses us from all sin. By confessing our sins and *believing* that God has cleansed us—because His word tells us so—we can know we are clean, and our feelings will soon catch up with our belief. This is how we come out of the dark shadows and into the light!

God showed me that legalism—my "performing" to gain His acceptance—was equivalent to the leaf aprons Adam and Eve made to cover their shame. My legalistic performance, like the aprons, was completely insufficient. God provided animal skin clothes for Adam and Eve—which meant that an animal substitute shed its blood to cover their sin. This was a preview of how Jesus Christ would give up His life and shed His blood to take away my sin. Only Jesus' blood is sufficient.

I have to admit that when I first realized my legalistic living was really lack of trust in Jesus, I was devastated. I felt so ashamed! I had to get on my face and ask God if I'd really ever been saved at all! But when I confessed my sin and surrendered my shame, He assured me, "Marcia, I hung naked on the cross to take your shame so you wouldn't have to bear it."

God didn't show me these things to devastate me. He wanted to set me free from all bondage in every form and disguise. He had to expose my core beliefs. He helped me see that, just as Adam and Eve had acted on their core belief about Him, I had always acted on mine. Immersing myself in His word became more crucial than ever—to change my core beliefs.

The more I came to know God, the more I could see that, because of who He is, there is absolutely never a need to feel lack. "The Lord is my Shepherd; I shall not want" (Ps. 23:1). I shall not lack! This revelation penetrated my heart deeply. God is everything I need, everything I could possibly want! As my Shepherd, He cares for me, protects me, and leads me.

Another verse also became a deep revelation: "Trust in the Lord with *all* your heart, and lean not on your own understanding. In *all* your ways, acknowledge Him, and He shall direct your paths" (Prov. 3:5, emphasis added). To stop acting independently of God, I had to give Him all my heart. To give Him all my heart, I had to trust Him. And to trust Him, I had to know Him—through His word and His Spirit.

Jesus came so that we *can* know God, and we can know that in every problem or circumstance He is more than enough. He's much more!

As I continued in His word, God went deeper and deeper into my old core beliefs that didn't match up with His truth, and deeper and deeper into my heart to reach the unhealed emotional wounds. As I confessed each wrong belief and gave each wound to Him, He healed me and changed me, and I reacted to lack less and less frequently. God was transforming my life.

God Has Not Given Us a Spirit of Fear

In October 2007, I began to go to the jail every Saturday night to share God's word with the women. As the weeks passed, I came to realize that the jail itself was a symbol of their spiritual bondage, just as the ashram had been of mine. Most of the women were enslaved to Satan through their use of drugs and witchcraft, and they admitted that they used drugs to numb their emotional pain. Their unhealed emotional wounds were snares the evil one used continually to maintain control over their lives. The feeling of lack led to sin, and sin led to more unbelief. I knew from what God had shown me from Genesis chapter three that they were reluctant to reach out to God because of fear and shame. Far too many of them remained trapped by the same lie Eve believed: "You can't trust God to do good for you, so you must rely on yourself, your own ways, and your own efforts." Most of them were so discouraged they had reached a paralyzing level of hopelessness. They couldn't fathom that the change they desperately wanted would come from reading and believing a book—the Bible.

I saw a few women who were nearly ready to believe in Jesus, but they needed the power of God immediately in their lives for healing and deliverance. I yearned for the power of God in their lives. Jesus gave His disciples authority over all the power of the evil one, and He said of those who would believe in Him, "They will lay hands on the sick, and they will recover" (Mark 16:18). The more I hungered for deliverance in the women's lives, the more I was tired of limiting God through my fear of the supernatural. Even though He was healing my heart layer by layer, this nagging fear held on because of my past relationship with the demon. I prayed for God to deliver me from my limiting thinking, and I fully expected Him to take care of my fear. He went even deeper

Chapter Six

than that—to a foundational layer of hopelessness that I didn't even know was in my heart.

In August 2008, God began to show me I was still being controlled by this old emotional habit that had developed during the decades I had been depressed and suicidal—this lingering attitude of hopelessness. Depression and suicidal thoughts were no longer a problem, but my expectation of receiving God's goodness in this life was low because of this dismal underlying layer of despair. It was like an invisible weight constantly dragging me down, but I'd become so used to it that I didn't realize it was there. The Holy Spirit revealed that because "faith is the substance of things hoped for," hope is absolutely necessary for faith to grow (Heb. 11:1). I began to pray that He would take the hopelessness out of my heart and replace it with His truth.

Later that month I attended a conference in a nearby city. One of the speakers invited each of us who needed physical healing to stand up, put our own hands on the body part that needed to be healed, and simply receive God's healing. I had lived for thirty-three years with migraine headaches. The daily pain was part of the weight of hopelessness. It was hard to imagine living any other way. But God's Spirit said to stand up—that it was time for my head to be healed. I stood up, put my hand on the right side of my head, and received. Instantly I was healed!

On another night of the conference, the speaker invited anyone dealing with fear to go up front for prayer. The Holy Spirit literally caused a pounding on the inside of my chest, just as if a finger was prodding me, "Go, go!" I hesitated a moment as the speaker listed specific fears. I argued with the Spirit, "But I'm not afraid of those things." The opportunity passed. Afterward I knew I had missed it and grieved the Holy Spirit. But it wasn't until I was driving home that I realized I had missed my opportunity to take care of the fear I'd carried for over eleven years—the fear of the supernatural. I prayed for a second chance all the way home. While I was driving and praying, the Holy Spirit revealed that I'd had the authority in Jesus' name to rebuke the spirit of fear all along. I did so right then, thanked God, and rejoiced. But God had even more in store.

The next day, the last of the conference, one speaker was talking with a few people in the lobby. I overheard someone ask him why Christians are so afraid to walk in the supernatural gifts of the Spirit. This question caught my interest! I stood in the back of the group and listened. The speaker stayed with us for quite a while. Before he left he prayed with us, and my faith soared. I knew I was delivered from the fear of the supernatural. When he finished, he looked at me and said, "I believe God wants to use some of you standing here in a supernatural ministry soon."

Later that afternoon, God made a way for me to speak with several other women at the conference, one by one. We shared our personal stories, and for the first time I shared openly with other believers about my fear of the supernatural. I wasn't used to having this kind of fellowship. Always before, I had kept all this hidden away inside, as if to protect myself from condemnation and rejection I feared I would receive if other believers knew. But each woman asked to hear more about my past, and the more I spoke about it, the more it seemed that light was shining on the fear, a light that made it shrink to nothing. Through the love these women shared, I gained freedom I had never known. And the love God had just poured into me was about to overflow.

The next evening I went to the jail. God's presence was powerfully manifested in a thick, almost-tangible love, and, although I'd never done it before, I laid hands on some of the women who needed physical healing. As they were healed of physical ailments and relieved of pain, they were deeply moved. Some wept at His word, and many were saved. All were deeply affected by His presence. They spontaneously broke out in songs of praise to God and didn't want to leave when "church" was over (quite unusual at the jail).

In the following weeks, God continued to manifest His healing in more and more women. Back pain, a broken foot, neck and shoulder problems, and other physical needs bowed to the name of Jesus. But it wasn't only physical ailments. Some women needed to be delivered from demon spirits of depression, discouragement, addiction, and perversion. When I prayed in the authority of Jesus' name, the spirits left. Each week, more women were saved and baptized in the Holy Spirit.

God confirmed His word to the women at the jail by signs and healings, and I watched some of them be transformed. Some, who had been contentious and unloving, softened and expressed love instead of hostility as weeks went by. Others who had been enslaved to drugs were delivered and strengthened in faith. They trusted God's power to keep them clean as they left for prison or home. Some developed an extraordinary hunger for God's word. All this was because the gospel had come to them not "in word only, but in power, and in the Holy Spirit and in much assurance" (1 Thes. 1:5).

My level of hope skyrocketed! But as it shot up, it also went down deep to act as a jackhammer, busting up that old crusty layer of hopelessness and disbelief in my heart. For the first time ever, I really believed that I could do all things through Christ who strengthens me (Phil. 4:13).

Then in September 2008, I spent three days in the city where I'd lived twenty-five years earlier—where I'd gone to law school and married Steve—to participate in street evangelism. On the last day, I was downtown speaking with people at bus stops, partnered with a gentleman named Joe. We stayed within eyesight of each other, but roamed about freely to talk to as many people as we could. About two o'clock, I noticed a woman sitting in a wheelchair in the portico of the Federal Building, taking shelter from the rain. The Holy Spirit said, "Go to her," so I did.

I introduced myself, and we began to talk. Her name was Trisha, and she was very troubled that day. Her Social Security check had been stolen, and she and her family were going to be evicted because she couldn't pay the rent. Somehow, even in these circumstances, the Holy Spirit prompted me to tell her about

Jesus before I prayed for her situation. She prayed to receive Jesus as her Savior.

Then the Holy Spirit urged me to ask about her body—why she was in a wheelchair. She told me she'd had a stroke and couldn't walk. She had on sandals, and I could see that the toes on her right foot were curled under. The fingers on her right hand were also curled into a fist. Suddenly, I was filled with total assurance that she was going to walk then and there. The Holy Spirit filled me with faith, and I asked her if I could pray for her body. She said yes, so I went to the back of the wheelchair, put my hand on her head, and commanded the effects of the stroke to be reversed in the name of Jesus. When I opened my eyes, she was moving and flexing the fingers of her right hand in front of her face. I said, "Trisha, can you do anything you couldn't do before?"

She said, "Yeah—this!"

I went to the front of her wheelchair, kicked up the footplates, held out my hands, and said, "The Lord says to you, 'Rise up and walk!'" The gift of faith was working in me. It was as if the Holy Spirit was telling me exactly what to do, and I was doing it as He said it.

But Trisha refused. She said she had tried to walk before and had always fallen. She didn't want to fall on the concrete.

I ran a few steps toward the bus stop where Joe was standing and yelled for him. He came running, and so did a police officer.

I assured Trisha that she would not fall, but if she didn't accept her healing by walking then and there, the devil could steal it. She got up out of the wheelchair with Joe at one elbow and me at the other. She took a few steps, then a few more. Then she jerked her arms away from us and walked on her own, with the policeman watching the whole thing. When I asked her how it felt to be walking, she said, "Pretty good!"

After Trisha walked around the portico for a few minutes, she sunk back into her chair, remembering her financial plight.

Again, the Holy Spirit gave me an unusual assurance—that one of her sons would find the money they needed on his way home. Joe and I prayed about this, gave Trisha some follow-up materials, then moved on to pray with others.

I never saw or talked to Trisha again, so I honestly don't know for sure how things turned out for her. However, I know that God did not spare His own Son, but delivered Him up for her. So, I'm sure He would freely give her the rent money she needed (Rom. 8:32)!

That evening when we returned to the convention center, I told one of the ministers about Trisha. The minister asked, "How many people have you prayed with to receive the Lord in the days you've been with us?"

"Ninety-nine."

"Ninety-nine?! You've got to make it one hundred!"

Another minister dialed a pizza place on his cell phone and handed it to me. When I began to talk about Jesus to the young woman who answered, she hung up. The minister dialed another pizza place, and another young woman answered. She put me on hold.

The praise and worship service had begun, and it was hard to hear, so I took the cell phone to a restroom. I was tempted to hang up after five minutes or so. Then I heard a young man's voice.

"Hi, welcome to Panjoe's Pizza. This is Stephen. Would you like to try our special this evening?"

"No, thank you, Stephen, but if I could, I'd like to ask you a very important question. Has anyone ever told you that God loves you and has a wonderful plan for your life?"

The tone of Stephen's voice changed completely—he was serious, attentive, and even reverent. I explained the gospel to Stephen, and he prayed to receive Jesus Christ as His Lord and Savior. I couldn't give him any follow-up materials, so I spoke with him briefly about finding a church and reading the Bible to feed his spirit and renew his mind. He thanked me for talking to him and said he would do these things.

By the time I finished the conversation, the worship service was in full swing. My heart was overflowing with joy! Even with the loud praise band I heard the still small voice of God explain that I was feeling His heart, the heart that rejoices over the one even more than the ninety-nine (Luke 15:4-7).

It wasn't until hours later that the full significance of the day's events dawned on me. As I was singing praises to God on the drive home through the night, He showed me: I had been in the city where Steve and I had lived twenty-five years before, walking the same streets we had walked—where I had spoken unkind words to "Bible-thumpers." Transformed into a Bible-thumper myself, I'd seen ninety-nine people saved on those streets, and I would have been satisfied. But because a minister pushed me beyond my expectations, another life had been changed forever—and his name was Stephen! The Holy Spirit had prepared the young man's heart for that moment—the moment that had been known in God's heart since before time began.

I couldn't help but praise Him more! My God is the God of comfort and hope, and He is the God who forgives! How many times had I rejected Him? I had lived in a pit of despair and even went so far as to be controlled by a demon. But He reached down to me in grace and mercy, made me new, and gave me His Spirit! God didn't give me a spirit of fear! He gave me His Spirit of power and of love and of a sound mind (2 Tim. 1:7)!

Then, in quiet reflection, I considered Steve—my Steve. God is so merciful, isn't it possible that He revealed Himself in Steve's heart before his death? Was the phone call to Stephen at the pizza place some kind of sign that somehow my Steve was OK—in heaven? I asked. Instead of hearing a direct answer, I was flooded with an awareness of God's goodness. His love and goodness are like an ocean, which He freely pours into our lives. His mercy endures forever, and His judgments are right. He is righteous in all His ways. Since that night, I've been untroubled

Chapter Six

by any questions about Steve. It's not that my love for him has diminished or my concern for his eternal destiny has waned. I simply trust God's goodness.

Chapter Seven

~ ~ ~

Accepted in the Beloved

By October 2008, I'd spent nineteen months in God's intensive care—the best months of my life. He had peeled back the layers of my heart, one by one, freeing me from guilt, condemnation, legalism, fear and hopelessness—barriers that had kept me from living the life Jesus died to give me. Each time He had prepared my heart with a deeper revelation of His love and had arranged my circumstances to bring me to a place of surrender. His timing had been perfect. Now it was time for Him to reach the tender center of my heart.

I was attending a church where there was great freedom in worship. Sunday after Sunday, reverent yet uninhibited worship welcomed the presence of God. Time didn't matter. The order of service didn't matter. We just poured out our hearts in worship and let Him do His work. In His manifest presence, I was restored in ways words can barely describe. Looking back, I see that God was preparing my heart. I was learning to receive from Him as a child receives from a loving Father—simply standing before Him, open and unashamed. I didn't have to figure out what I needed or carefully use the right words to ask for it. He knew, and He gave.

But at the same time, during October, I was trying to prepare materials for a seminar scheduled for Saturday the 25th at a women's prison. The title of the seminar was supposed to be "Winning the Victory," and I wanted to share the teaching God had given me from Genesis chapter three—how the process

The Heart-*Changer*

of sin starts with the feeling of lack, and how the antidote is to trust God and run to Him with every need. This revelation had certainly won the victory for me many times after I'd received it. But every time I sat down to write the materials there seemed to be some kind of weight on me, and I became sluggish, tired, and discouraged. I was tempted to cancel the seminar.

By the morning of Sunday the 19th, I still hadn't prepared the materials, but I had recognized that a spirit of discouragement was the problem. I prayed in the authority of Jesus' name, and others at church prayed with me. I knew the spirit had no authority over me. Still, I felt something holding me back. The struggle wasn't over.

At the evening service, we sang a song I had come to love: "There is a fountain filled with grace, and it flows from Emmanuel's veins! It came and healed me, it came and refreshed me, it came and washed my sins away! I will rejoice, I will rejoice, and be glad!"[6] I stood in God's presence, wanting to receive from Him, but whatever was holding me back prevented it. I prayed in the Spirit, and a few moments later the pastor said, "Come on, you know you've never really been glad you're alive." Instantly, by the power of the Holy Spirit, I realized that, at my core, I still regretted my existence. Yes, God had long ago delivered me from the deep depression that had characterized my life in earlier years. He had freed me from the suicidal thoughts that had plagued me. But I still wasn't filled with joy simply to be alive. It was the oldest and deepest hurt of my life, from the first lie I'd ever believed—that my life was a dreadful mistake. I lifted my hands and gave it to God. The Holy Spirit whispered, "Always accepted, never rejected." Immediately I knew He was referring to the passage in Ephesians He had wanted me to believe ten years earlier: "To the praise of the glory of His grace, by which He made us accepted in the Beloved" (Eph. 1:6). Tears flowed as I confessed that, deep in my heart, I'd never really believed I was accepted. His fountain of grace poured out forgiveness. But there was still more to come.

Chapter Seven

God strengthened me to finish the materials in time for the seminar at the prison. About halfway into the two hour drive early that morning, the Holy Spirit asked, "Do you know why Satan has tried to stop you from going to the prison to teach this seminar?" As usual, He gave me the answer in my heart. The resistance I'd encountered was because I was about to expose Satan's strategy to women he had so successfully oppressed in the past. By the grace of God, I was about to hand them a key to their inner prisons! I shouted for joy and sang the rest of the way.

That day the other volunteers, the inmates, and I rejoiced with rousing praise and worship, singing of God's favor and of our new identity in Christ. Then, the women became quiet as I shared the message—how the feeling of lack sets us up to be self-focused rather than God-focused. I explained how the devil uses this one strategy in different situations, and the women saw it: the argumentative bunkmate, the rejection letter from home, and the unappetizing meal in the cafeteria are really the same—temptation to think, "*This* time it's different. *This* time I'm justified in doing things my way. God can't handle *this*." In small groups they began to recognize this pattern in their past. And, most importantly, they saw that the answer is to stay close to God at all times—to run to Him, where there is no lack. Their response was so positive, I thought, "I couldn't be happier."

After the seminar, a delightful young woman came to see me. When she shared her story, I could see that our childhood backgrounds were so similar. She requested prayer for the deep rejection she'd carried in her heart all her life, so that she could love others more. I prayed the very words the Holy Spirit had given me the previous Sunday evening, that she would receive a deep revelation that she is "always accepted, never rejected." Then she sweetly said, "Lord, I pray the very same thing for Marcia."

The next morning at church we sang the same songs I had taken to the prison. The music opened up a floodgate of joy in my heart as I praised our victorious God. The presence of the Lord fell heavily as we worshiped, and a woman prophesied that God would make "mountains melt like wax" (Ps. 97:5).

There was a drama that evening at church, and the final scene depicted believers meeting Jesus in heaven. The worship was beautiful, and the loving, healing presence of God was so strong—strong enough to melt mountains like wax! And that's exactly what happened. Standing in His presence, unashamedly letting tears flow, I was enveloped in His love—love so strong and so deep that nothing opposing it could stand. The mountain of rejection I'd carried in my heart since childhood melted. God healed the deepest hurt in my heart, and He did it in a way that only He could do—He melted my heart and expanded it by His love.

For a while, I celebrated this event as another new beginning in my life, as if it had been that event on that day, when I had *felt* the love of God so strongly, that the tormenting sense of rejection had been defeated. But as I continued in God's word, He enabled me to realize that my rejection had really been defeated in eternity past—when He chose me before the foundation of the world, as He says in Ephesians. He helped me understand that when Jesus hung on the cross—despised and rejected by men and forsaken by God, for my sake—He delivered the fatal blow to rejection. Jesus rose from the dead to give me newness of life, a life filled with the joy of knowing God, my accepting Father! What happened the evening of the church drama was that God's mercy and love conquered my unbelief, revealing the heart of my Father, who runs after me until all that is wrong in me melts in His embrace.

There is None Like God

Later, when I reflected again on all that God had done in my life, I realized that from March 2007, when I entered His intensive care, to October 2008, when He healed my deepest emotional wound, was nineteen months—the same amount of time I'd spent in the ashram a decade earlier, when I still labored under the delusion that I could change myself. This is God—the Heart-Changer! He is able to do what no other can do! He is God Most High, yet He loves to be so involved in our lives that He takes notice of even the smallest wisp of thought in our minds. He is God, needing to prove Himself to no one, yet because of His love He does. He has proven Himself in my life in so many ways!

It reminds me of how God proved Himself in the time of Elijah the prophet. The people of Israel had never completely forgotten about God, but on a day-to-day basis they worshiped and relied on a false god called Baal. Elijah challenged them, "How long will you hesitate between the two? If the Lord is God, then follow Him; if Baal, then follow him. Let's set up two altars with two sacrifices. You call on Baal, and I'll call on the Lord. The God who answers by fire, He is God" (1 Kings 18:21-24, author's paraphrase). Hundreds of the false god's priests prayed and danced around their sacrifice for hours. They even cut themselves, shedding their own blood, in an attempt to get a response from Baal. But their efforts were useless. Then Elijah set up his altar with a sacrifice and dug a trench around it. He poured many gallons of water on the wood and the sacrifice, so much that the water filled the trench. Then He prayed:

> "Hear me, O Lord, hear me, that this people may know that You are the Lord God, and that You have turned their hearts back to You again." Then the fire of the Lord fell and consumed the burnt sacrifice, and the wood and the stones and the dust, and it licked up the water that was in the trench (1 Kings 18:37-38).

God has not changed. He is the same God who answers by fire—even in the hearts of those who trust Him and stay close to Him!

> If Christ is to make me what I am to be, I must tarry in fellowship with God. If God is to let His love enter in and shine and burn through my heart, I must take time to be with Him. The blacksmith puts his rod of iron into the fire. If he leaves it there for only a short amount of time, it does not become red hot. He may take it out to do something with it and, after a time, put it back again for a few minutes, but this time it does not become red hot either. In the course of the day, he may put the rod into the fire a great many times and leave it there for two or three minutes each time. But it never becomes thoroughly heated. If he takes his time and leaves the rod in the fire for ten or fifteen minutes, the whole iron will become red-hot from the fire's heat. So if we are to have the fire of God's holiness and love and power, we must spend more time with God in fellowship.[7]

This is why I will *never* leave God's "intensive care unit"! It's not a short-term fix; it's a way of life.

Since October 2008, God has taught me how to remain in His intensive care in all kinds of circumstances. He slowly nudged me back into full-time work while still enjoying lots of time in His presence and His word. I continued in the cleaning job through 2009, with added bursts of activity here and there—teaching Sunday school at a large church, presenting another in-prison seminar, and helping a woman released from prison. In January 2010, God provided a new job—teaching at a small college—to replace the cleaning job. Then, beginning in the spring of 2010, He provided a tremendously rewarding opportunity as a volunteer helping to establish a Christ-centered residential center for women with life-controlling problems in a community seventy miles away. My life became very challenging and quite busy, not only with the traveling, but also with helping in all that needed

Chapter Seven

to be done—from cleaning, to planning, to researching, and, eventually, to serving as a weekend "house-mom" to residents who were being set free from substance abuse. The demanding pace was worth it to see God prove Himself in their lives just as He had done in mine. As these women immersed themselves in God's word and spent time in His presence, they found their lives being healed—layer by layer.

And to my surprise, it was while I was researching to gain a better understanding of substance abuse that I gained a key insight into the bliss I'd experienced in meditation in 1994. It has to do with the way God created the human brain.

Our thoughts and feelings result from messages sent from nerve cell to nerve cell inside our brains. These messages are communicated by certain chemicals, which scientists call neurotransmitters because they transmit messages between nerve cells, or neurons. As a particular neurotransmitter is released by one cell, it attaches to the next cell by fitting into a specially-shaped receptor. Messages travel through the brain by going from one neuron to another along the nerve pathways.

God has hard-wired our brains for pleasure! Yes, God placed in the center of our brains a structure which scientists call the "reward pathway," because the messages that pass through these nerve cells reward life-sustaining behaviors with feelings of pleasure. When the reward pathway functions the way God intended, we feel pleasure when, for example, we eat a good meal or drink a refreshing glass of ice water on a hot day.

But when drugs interfere, the reward pathway is flooded with too much of the brain chemicals that produce feelings of pleasure—resulting in a "high." How do drugs interfere? They mimic, or counterfeit, the neurotransmitters in our brains. They fit into the receptors meant for our God-given neurotransmitters and don't let go, so the pleasure-producing chemicals are dumped out in larger doses. The counterfeits "lie" to brain cells and make them react in ways God didn't intend, taking people down a

The Heart-*Changer*

path that feels good for a while, but eventually leads to bondage, sorrow, and death.[8]

Drugs are just an extension of the original lie Satan told Eve in the Garden of Eden: "You can't count on God to do good for you. You've got a need He can't fill, so you need to take care of it yourself." When a person feels lack—such as from a problem in a relationship, the loss of a loved one, or emotional pain from the past—and turns to drugs, she is falling for the same old lie in a different disguise. Worse yet, drugs wind up creating a feeling of lack all their own—addictive cravings for more. The drugs may numb the feeling of lack temporarily (*very* temporarily), but they won't fill the real need, and there will only be more lack!

So, what's the answer? It's described in the Bible: "In Your presence is fullness of joy; at Your right hand are pleasures forevermore" (Ps. 16:11). The answer is pleasure, the very thing God has hard-wired us for. But it's pleasure in His presence—joy that can be felt only in the presence of God. His answer for the drug addict is to become addicted to His presence—to real pleasure instead of the counterfeit. In Him there is no lack. And how can we—who have sinned and are so unworthy to be near God—how can we come into His presence where there is fullness of joy? We can enter boldly because of the blood Jesus shed for our sins on the cross!

What does this have to do with the bliss I experienced in meditation? One day in my research on drugs and the brain, I came across the name of a neurotransmitter that grabbed my attention: anandamide. This name struck me because I recognized its root, *ananda*, as the Sanskrit word meaning bliss. Anandamide is known to scientists as "the bliss molecule." It's one of the body's natural means of controlling pain and depression.[9]

This discovery led to questions: Were my bliss experiences simply a result of the evil one's manipulation of my neurotransmitters? If Satan uses drugs to manipulate human neurotransmitters, could he not do the same through meditation? I'm not a scientist, and I have no means to prove the answer to these questions, but I believe the answer is yes. When I rejected Jesus and chose to meditate in 1994, I allowed demonic influence over my neurotransmitters. Just as drugs counterfeit real pleasure, the bliss in meditation was a counterfeit of God's real joy. After all, I was as "hooked" on meditation as an addict is on drugs. I had to have it; and if I didn't, I endured intense cravings. When I stopped kriya yoga in 1997, the physical pain and anguish was very much like the withdrawal symptoms of a drug addict.

So, what does this all mean? It means the story of my life is just like the story of an addict. I started at a young age using self-pity to escape the pain of rejection and depression, and as an adult I moved on to the "hard stuff." The temporary relief that came from meditation was like the high of drugs, and the end was the same—bondage to Satan, whose purpose was to kill me and rob me of eternal life with God.

But it also means that using drugs is just as much idolatry as my bowing down to pictures of gurus at the ashram. Replacing the true and living God with *anything* is idolatry. God wants us to run to Him with our pain and problems. He tells us to cast all these on Him because He cares for us (1 Pet. 5:7). When we turn to drugs, or bliss in meditation, or food, or relationships, or anything but God, we become idolaters.

And it means that turning to the "god of one's own understanding" to get off drugs is as futile as my turning to self-help books to change my heart. It's useless. The "god of one's own understanding" is a false god created in one's own sin-infected heart.

Most importantly, it means that the cure for the addict, or any other idolater, is the same as it was for me—the pleasure, the unspeakable joy that comes from being in the presence of God. And thanks to the saving sacrifice of Jesus Christ, this cure is available to all who put their faith in Him. There is none like God, ready to save all who call out to Him for mercy, ready to fill their hearts with joy.

The Heart-*Changer*

Heart-Changing Joy

This heart-changing joy goes beyond feelings. It doesn't depend on good circumstances. It is a joy that's there whether one is on the highest mountain-top of gladness or in the lowest valley of sorrow. It's there in the face of failure and pain. It is a joy that remains no matter how one's future on earth is affected by one's decisions in the past. It stands firmly in the knowledge that God is faithful: "My God is for me, not against me. He will never leave me; He will never, never, never forsake me" (Rom. 8:31; Heb. 13:5).

This heart-changing joy is all of the above and more—but joy itself is *not* God. It is not something to be pursued for its own sake. No, this joy is a fruit, or a result, of God's Holy Spirit living inside the person who has been born again. It's a result of God's pursuing us!

Jesus told a parable about a father and son to help us see how God pursues us. One day the son told his father, "I can't wait long enough for you to die. Give me my share of your estate now, and let me be on my way." The father let the boy have what he wanted, and the son went off to a far country and blew every last dime partying. He wasted it all and had nothing to show for it. Times got really bad, and with no friends to be found, the son became very hungry. The young man had no choice but to get a dirty job feeding pigs. He was so hungry that he was jealous of the pigs for their slop. When he'd hit bottom, he suddenly came to himself and said, "Wait! My father has more than enough. Even dad's hired servants are well-fed, and here I am starving. I'll get up and go back to my father, and say, 'Father, I have sinned against heaven and against you. I'm not worthy to be your son, but please let me be like one of your hired servants.'" The young man set out on his journey home, but even when he was still a long way off he saw something he never expected. His father was running to him! His father had been waiting and watching, and before the son could even get close to home, the father ran to embrace him. The son sputtered out, "Father, I've sinned against heaven and against you, and I'm not worthy to be your son," but that's as much as the father would let him say. Overjoyed, the father yelled out orders to the servants, "Bring the best robe in the house, and put it on my son! Bring a ring, and put it on his finger! Put sandals on his feet, and prepare a celebration dinner! For my son was dead, but now he's alive! He was lost, but now he's found!" (Luke 15:13-24, author's paraphrase).

The son in this parable is a picture of us with our sin-infected hearts—indifferent to God, wanting His "stuff" but not Him, and wanting to do things our own way without His interference. We inherited hearts like this from our first ancestors. The Bible says that even though Adam was created in God's image, after Adam sinned, his children were born in his image (Gen. 5:1-3). What a change for the worse! But God didn't change. He created mankind with the freedom to choose because He wanted true love, freely given. God is still the same today. He will let us have what we want, even if it means we eventually hit bottom. Then, when we see the horror, futility, and foolishness of our sin and stop blaming others for it, He changes our hearts so that we want to return to Him.

The father in the parable is a picture of God's attitude toward us when we come to Him. He rejoices over us! He doesn't throw our track record up in our faces to make us feel worse. He doesn't punish us. He welcomes us with open arms, embraces us, and restores us. He can do this because of everything Jesus has done for us.

The desire of God's heart is for every person to come to Him. He is "not willing that any should perish but that all should come to repentance" (2 Pet. 3:9). "Repentance" may at first seem like an old-fashioned word, and it's certainly not a popular word in today's world. But God's goodness leads us to repentance (Rom. 2:4). Actually, it is a gift of God, part of His giving us faith to believe. God opens our eyes so that we see Him and ourselves in a realistic light—to see how we have spurned Him to go our own way, despite all His kindness and goodness toward us. Because we loved ourselves more than God, we didn't acknowledge His rightful claim on us. Once we see this, we agree with God about all that our sin should get for us, and we say, "You are blameless when You judge me, God, and You are right to condemn me" (Ps. 51:4, author's paraphrase). It is a heart-crushing realization to know that our sin is against *God*—our good and kind Creator. But it is when our hearts are so crushed that we begin to know the extent of His goodness and grace. Even though He would be completely just in condemning us and punishing us forever, He won't, because Jesus has already suffered in our place so that we can be free. And He changes our hearts so that we desire to use our freedom to live only for Him.

If we look very closely at the picture this parable gives us, we'll see that there is a point in time when we realize we can't help ourselves and say, "I'll go to God." This change of heart is a gift from God, which He brings about by His Holy Spirit. And there's a moment when God says, "You were dead, but now you're alive." This gift of new life, too, is brought about by the Holy Spirit, who comes to live inside us when we are born again.

The Bible points out that one person can't really know what another is like deep inside. Only the person's spirit really knows. And no one really knows the things of God except the Spirit of God. The Holy Spirit searches and knows even the deep things of God (1 Cor. 2:10-11). And *this* is the Spirit God shares with us! *This* is the Spirit He sends to live in us!

> Do you not know that you are the temple of God and that the Spirit of God dwells in you? (1 Cor. 3:16)

> Or do you not know that your body is the temple of the Holy Spirit who is in you, whom you have from God, and you are not your own? (1 Cor. 6:19)

> But he who is joined to the Lord is one spirit with Him (1 Cor. 6:17).
>
> And what agreement has the temple of God with idols? For you are the temple of the living God. As God has said: "I will dwell in them and walk among them. I will be their God, and they shall be My people" (2 Cor. 6:16).

This is why Jesus could say that eternal life is knowing God (John 17:3)—because we *can* know the one true and living God if His Spirit lives in us! We don't need a "god of our own understanding." God reveals Himself by His word and His Spirit. We can know *Him*.

Self-improvement, self-help, and self-realization promise us everything from feeling better to being merged with God, but these are false promises. In fact, they're just extensions of the original lie Satan told Eve in the Garden of Eden, "You will be like God, knowing good and evil," as if we, on our own without God, can know what is good. We can't. God is the Creator, and we are the created. We must rely on Him to know anything, including Himself and ourselves.

True Christianity not only promises, but also delivers, union with God in Jesus Christ through the Holy Spirit.

> At that day you will know that I am in My Father, and you in Me, and I in you. He who has my commandments and keeps them, it is he who loves Me. And he who loves Me will be loved by My Father, and I will love him and manifest Myself to him (John 14:20-21).

Think of it! God shares Himself with us! When we come to Him for salvation, He doesn't put us on probation to see how we'll do. He doesn't wait. He gives us Himself. He can do this because of all that Jesus did on the cross—He took away our sin, so that we can be a clean and holy dwelling place for His Spirit.

> What then shall we say to these things? If God is for us, who can be against us? He who did not spare His own Son, but delivered Him up for us all, how shall He not with Him also freely give us all things? (Rom. 8:31-32)

Just like the father who quickly ordered the finest robe for his son, God wraps us in robes of righteousness. He restores us to the Father-child relationship, just as the father in the parable immediately put the ring on his son's finger. And just as the father had sandals put on the young man's feet to signify that he was not a slave but a son, God puts His Spirit in us, lavishing His love and grace on us! *This* is the source of heart-changing joy—that we *know God*!

Chapter Eight

~ ~ ~

True Freedom

Throughout 2009 and most of 2010, I lived in celebration of what I thought was true freedom. God had healed my heart's wounds, and I was truly happy. I lived to enjoy and worship God, the more vigorously the better. The more I worshiped, the happier I was. But to a large degree, I was living as though the ultimate goal of everything God had done for me was my own happiness—as if it was the be all and end all.

My relationship with God was better than ever because my fear of the supernatural, fear of rejection, and feelings of condemnation were gone; but I began to notice that my obedience, many times, was at my convenience. Yes, of course, since it was God, it was at my *earliest* convenience. But, still, I treated God almost as if I were His equal—as if He was another lawyer or a judge, and I could negotiate with Him. As long as I got around to doing what He asked before His absolute drop-deadline, it was all right.

Even if I didn't show it outwardly, I felt superior to other believers whom I deemed below "my level of spirituality," almost as if I was a part of Jesus' "in crowd" as opposed to the other wannabes. Sometimes I was impatient with the women at the jail. I'm ashamed to admit it, but my attitude at times was, "After all, if these folks would just apply themselves (like *me*!), they could 'get it' (like *me*!)."

And as God was giving me more opportunities to serve Him in public settings, I found myself wanting to be noticed. Oh, it was even better if I was noticed for doing a good job, but just to be noticed was quite nice—to be seen as the "super-Christian" I was.

I began to wonder why—if my heart, even the rejection in the tender center, had been healed—why did I still react to some people in such a cold, defensive way? Why was I only capable of a formal, obligatory kind of love toward them? What was still in me that prevented a completely spontaneous, genuine love?

None of these attitudes became obvious to me all at once, and I certainly didn't see the totality of them at any one given time. I couldn't have noticed any of them without God's Word and His Holy Spirit. But God is faithful to His promises, and one of them is that He will finish the good work He started in me (Phil. 1:6). It turned out that by taking all the layers off my heart, God had exposed the real problem—my "self." It was still all about me.

Gradually, over the months, the Holy Spirit pointed out these wrong attitudes. When I was straining to be noticed, Jesus would remind me of how He washed the disciples' feet. He would take me back to His instructions to sit in the lowliest seat at any gathering. He brought back to my memory something God says again and again in the Scriptures: that He resists the proud but gives grace to the humble.

When I reacted coldly to people who had hurt me in the past—not necessarily rudely, but not with genuine warmth—Jesus would ask, "Is this how you would have Me treat you?" Where would I be if God forgave me, but still held me at arm's length?

God prepared my heart by taking me repeatedly to Jesus' words: "If anyone desires to come after Me, let him deny himself, and take up his cross daily, and follow Me" (Luke 9:23). I had read these words many times before, but now He put in me a hunger to know them deep in my heart.

Each time the Holy Spirit convinced me of my selfishness and self-focus, I prayed for forgiveness and to be set free—to be changed. And gradually there was some improvement. But there

Chapter Eight

came a moment in time when God would do something so big that it would give me the true freedom I'd always wanted.

It was one of the biggest moments of my life, but it came without fanfare or hoopla. There was no heart-tugging music, no tears. Nobody else was around to see it. God often does big things in quiet ways that seem small to us.

I was driving home one sunny afternoon in September 2010, quietly praying in the Spirit, and as I made a right turn about a half-mile from the house, the Holy Spirit urged me to pray this: "Father, I give up my right to act and react like Marcia, so that Jesus can live through me. Amen."

That was it. It doesn't seem like much, but next to the short prayer I prayed on March 22, 1998 ("Oh! Save me!"), it was the most important prayer of my life. It became a daily prayer.

Immediately I noticed a change in my relationships. All the little ways I used to draw back from people were simply leftovers, hanging on from earlier in life. They'd become so second nature that I thought they were permanent. But when I gave up my right to act and react like me, I was free—*truly* free.

In the first few weeks after this prayer, God really poured out His grace. It was easy to respond and act in new ways. Then, about the time I began to take it for granted, He backed off little by little—so that I would remain completely dependent on Him each moment for the grace I needed.

This true freedom affected every relationship in my life. My defensiveness and haughty attitude were replaced by genuine love and appreciation. It was truly a transformation only God could achieve.

I call this "true freedom" because I've learned that freedom isn't just enjoying myself and doing things that make me happy without the drag of old baggage. True freedom isn't escaping the company of people who may hurt me or get on my nerves. It isn't just mental assent to the truth, and it's not simply being forgiven of my sins, as greatly important as being forgiven is. True freedom is laying down my life and letting Jesus live through me. It's dying to my agenda and letting God's agenda be all. It's letting go of my excuses and preferences so that I can live Jesus' life of obedience. It's completely ceasing to be my own god, and letting God be my only God. True freedom is keeping God's commands.

> A new commandment I give to you, that you love one another; as I have loved you, that you also love one another. By this all will know that you are My disciples, if you have love for one another (John 13:34-35).

> For you, brethren, have been called to liberty; only do not use liberty as an opportunity for the flesh, but through love serve one another. For all the law is fulfilled in one word, even in this: "You shall love your neighbor as yourself" (Gal. 5:13-14).

> For though I am free from all men, I have made myself a servant to all, that I might win more (1 Cor. 9:19).

As much as God has transformed my life and enabled me to love and to obey His commands like never before, I still have a long way to go! How is it that the thought of keeping God's commands doesn't throw me back into the hopelessness I'd known for so many years—all those years I'd tried to be a better person, but just couldn't? How is it that keeping God's commands doesn't drag me down into legalism—where my relationship with Him hinges on my successful performance? If *ultimate freedom* is in keeping God's commandment to love, how can I be sure that I will always have it? These questions essentially ask the same thing the ladies in jail ask every Saturday night: "Is there anything that can keep me from going back to my old ways? I have so far to go; there's so much to change. How can I be sure that I'll be all God wants me to be?"

My time in God's intensive care had been spent focusing on "who I am in Christ." Up to this point, the emphasis had been on the "who I am" part. I am accepted in the Beloved, not rejected. I don't have a spirit of fear, but the Spirit of power, love, and a sound mind. There is no condemnation for those who are in Christ Jesus, so I am not condemned. And I am not under law, but under grace. I had come to believe these truths from the bottom of my heart, and they had changed my life. These truths had been the fire that melted each old layer from my heart to reveal my "self."

But now it was time to focus on the "in Christ" part of "who I am in Christ." If I am to die to myself and let Jesus live through me, I must know what it means to be *in Christ*. Jesus is the guarantee of eternal freedom. He's the security in a relationship with God. The more I know Jesus, the simpler life becomes. It really boils down to the word, *chesed*, and the song God brought to my memory years ago at the ashram:

> My hope is built on nothing less
> Than Jesus' blood and righteousness.
> I dare not trust the sweetest frame,
> But wholly lean on Jesus' name.

Jesus' Blood and Righteousness

When God brought this hymn to my mind back in 1997, I had no idea what the words meant. I knew that Jesus shed His blood when He died on the cross, but I didn't know why it was important. Soon after I came to know Jesus as my Savior, I realized there was a lot of emphasis on His blood in the songs we sang at church, and I read in the Bible about how His blood washed away my sins. But I sensed there was even more—much more that I had not yet grasped. Years later, after God removed the layers from my heart and exposed my "self," I developed a hunger to know: What is the power of Jesus' blood?

Centuries before Jesus was born on earth, God set up a system of animal sacrifices that would temporarily cover the sins of His people, and He emphasized the importance of the blood of these sacrifices: "the life of the flesh is in the blood" (Lev. 17:11). The people knew from history why blood was necessary. God had told Adam in the Garden of Eden that sin would result in death, and this was true for each generation after Adam. Each sin required a life in payment; every sin should have resulted in the sinner's death. But God allowed animal substitutes—animals which had to die because "the life was in the blood."

But the blood of animals couldn't really take away the sins of human beings; and God didn't want to be separated from His people forever because of their sin. This is why Jesus—God in human flesh—came to die on the cross.

The Gospel of John begins with these words:

> In the beginning was the Word, and the Word was with God, and the Word was God. He was in the beginning with God. All things were made through Him, and without Him nothing was made that was made. In Him was life, and the life was the light of men . . . And the Word became flesh and dwelt among us, and we beheld His glory, the glory as of the only begotten of the Father, full of grace and truth (John 1:1-4, 14).

"In Him was life." Jesus is the Source of all life. *In Him* is life itself—God's life. So the power and quality of God's life is the life that's in Jesus' blood. This is why His blood is sufficient not only to take away the sins *of* humankind, but also to conquer the power of sin *for* humankind. Jesus' life, death, and resurrection defeated sin and death.

But there is more. Jesus is God, but He also became a human being. So the life He lived as a human being is also in His blood. What kind of life did He live?

First and foremost, He lived a life of humble obedience to God His Father—always, "Not My will, but Yours be done." At all times, Jesus said and did only what the Father wanted Him to say and do. So Jesus' life of humility and obedience is in His blood.

Jesus lived a life of love and power. Even though He was God, He gave preference to those around Him. He lived to serve others and always relied on His Father to supply their needs, from healing incurable diseases to feeding thousands from just a sack lunch. Jesus' life of love and power is in His blood.

Jesus also lived a sinless life. He encountered every kind of temptation as Adam and Eve, and as all other humans, but He didn't sin. He never reacted to lack, but always trusted God His Father. He never acted independently of His Father, never turned to other people or things in place of His Father. As the first and only human being to live a life of perfect obedience, Jesus was victorious over sin. So His victorious life is in His blood.

In short, Jesus' life was pleasing to God the Father in all ways. *This* is the life that is in His blood. And the life of the risen Jesus is eternal—never dying, never slowing down, never decreasing in power. *This* is the life that is in His blood.

Here is some very good news: When we're born again, God sprinkles our new hearts with the blood of Jesus. When we are *in Christ*, His life is in us. The life in His blood is continuously applied to our hearts every moment of every day by the Holy Spirit. The blood that holds the very life of Jesus—the life of victory over sin, of love and power, of submission to the will of God, and of humble obedience—is in our hearts. And when we give up our right to act and react like ourselves, the life of Jesus comes out of our hearts—into our words and actions. His life overflows out of our hearts to others. The blood of Jesus changes our hearts so we can love God and others as He did!

Born again children of God never need worry that they don't have strength to live a life pleasing to God. Oh, yes, we are as weak as ever in ourselves, but God has given us all we need by the blood of Jesus. We have to receive it by faith, as a trusting child receives from a loving Father, and then live its truth, obeying His commands. When we have a feeling of lack and want to react in our old ways, we run to our Father with hearts sprinkled by the blood of Jesus, and the strength to live His life is ours. This is the power of grace! The power of sin is defeated in our lives!

Life with Jesus really comes down to the first real prayer I ever prayed to God. It was a prayer without words, when I cried out in my heart to God for *chesed* back in the ashram in 1997. I knew the word meant "lovingkindness," but I had no idea of its depth. *Chesed* is the Hebrew word that signifies life in covenant relationship with God.

Throughout history, God has entered into covenants with humankind. Long ago He made a covenant with the children of Israel, known as the old covenant. God pledged Himself and His blessings to them, and they pledged themselves to Him in obedience. They promised, "All that the Lord has said, we will do. We will be obedient." They knew this meant serious business. A covenant is an absolutely unbreakable promise. They were swearing on their own lives and the lives of their children for generations to come. But even as their promise was coming out of their mouths, God knew their sin-infected hearts weren't really in it. And, indeed, they broke the covenant again and again, generation after generation, by going their own way and worshiping other gods. They eventually suffered the consequences of their choices. Their temple was destroyed, and they were taken captive by their enemies because the terms of the old covenant required it. But God remained faithful to them, showing them mercy even though they had been unfaithful to Him. He didn't abandon them or allow them to be completely destroyed. He preserved them and brought them back to their land. This is

Chapter Eight

chesed—God's unbreakable covenant mercy and faithfulness, His unfailing and steadfast love.[10]

If we just knew God's *chesed* according to the old covenant, it would be something great. If we really believed God is faithful to us even when we're unfaithful to Him, how our lives would change! But the good news is that God offers us a new covenant that's based on even better promises than the old! In the new covenant, God takes the responsibility for His part *and* our part—because Jesus has already done our part. He obeyed perfectly for us and now lives in us, giving us His power to obey. This is what *chesed* means to us in the new covenant—God's unbreakable promise for the most loving, secure relationship possible. We can stay close to God without fear because Jesus represents us. He is our hope and our sure confidence. His own blood secures God's covenant with us. This is what it means to be *in Christ*.

It's important not to allow our past failures to keep us in a state of unbelief. There's a reason we failed in the past. We were born in the image of Adam with a heart set against God in stubborn pride and self-will. We were "in Adam" when he sinned, we are all descended from him, and his deceit-infected heart was passed down to each of us. From birth, we were in the same predicament as the children of Israel. No matter how many times we said, "I promise I will obey You, God," our deceit-infected hearts were powerless against sin. Our only hope is the new covenant in Jesus' blood.

How do we accept and enter into the new covenant? By faith, we believe *into* Jesus. Our physical lives began when we were born "in Adam," but when we are born again—*into* Christ—we lose our identity in Adam and gain a new identity in Christ. No longer slaves to our deceitful, self-willed hearts, we are "in Christ," our hearts sprinkled with the blood of Jesus—clean and empowered to obey God—so our past does not have to rule our future!

God's *chesed*—His unfailing love, faithfulness, and goodness toward us—began in His heart in eternity past, before He created the universe. He knew humankind would disobey and fall into sin. The Bible says that Jesus Christ is the Lamb slain from the foundation of the world (Rev. 13:8). Jesus' death and resurrection was God's plan all along—His plan to demonstrate His grace and mercy, His *chesed*. Yes, thousands of years passed between Adam's sin and Jesus' death on the cross, but His blood had secured God's *chesed* from eternity past. The power of Jesus' blood is eternal, without beginning or end.

And just as God had planned Jesus' death and resurrection before time began, He also planned that we who are "in Christ" will become like Him. This transformation takes time, but God's promise, secured by Jesus' blood, is that we will be like Him when we see Him face to face (1 John 3:2). Until then, He works in our hearts to transform us more and more into Jesus' image, day by day as we follow Him closely. And even though we sin and make mistakes along the way, He does not condemn us, because we are in Christ (Rom. 8:1).

God doesn't want us to give up because of our sin, mistakes, and failures. He wants us to remember that Jesus' blood guarantees that we ourselves will be pleasing to Him. His word tells us so:

> Now may the God of peace who brought up our Lord Jesus from the dead, that great Shepherd of the sheep, through the blood of the everlasting covenant, make you complete in every good work to do His will, working in you what is well pleasing in His sight, through Jesus Christ, to whom be glory forever and ever. Amen (Heb. 13:20-21).

This is a sure thing, not just a possibility. Look at the way believers are addressed in the Bible:

> Dear friends, God the Father chose you long ago and knew you would become His children. And

Chapter Eight

> the Holy Spirit has been at work in your hearts, cleansing you with the blood of Jesus Christ and making you to please Him. May God bless you richly and grant you increasing freedom from all anxiety and fear (1 Pet. 1:2 TLB).

God's promise to conform us to the image of His Son means that He will make our lives match up with Jesus' perfect life, the life He has put into our hearts. He has given us His victory. The blood of Jesus is the guarantee that God's promise will be fulfilled. We can believe it no matter what our circumstances might be at the moment.

The wonderful thing for people like me is that all this is true whether we understand at first or not. God's *chesed* is at work in our lives even when we don't realize it.

I now know that it was God's *chesed* that kept me alive as an infant, brought me to life after the car wreck, and later stopped my suicide plans. Because of His *chesed*, He remained faithful to me during all those years I rejected Him and even when I bowed down to other gods. It was the Holy Spirit who put it in my heart to pray for *chesed*—even to remember the word—when I was completely lost and blinded to God's truth. When I called out to God for *chesed*, I was actually praying to be brought into the new covenant through Jesus Christ, although I didn't even realize it at the time. And in March 1998, God's Spirit led me to pray *into* Jesus. God has been faithful to me since that night when I cried out to be saved, even through the years when I failed to obey and surrender. I am not the finished product God wants me to be, but I am confident that I will be—not because of my own willpower or strength, but because of God's *chesed*.

There *is* something that can keep us from going back to our old unloving ways, something true and secure, something that will never die or fade in power—the blood of Jesus. We can have the ultimate and true freedom of obeying God's commands—

because our hope is built on nothing less than Jesus' blood and righteousness!

And Now, Your Story

Think about your life. How many times has God protected you and preserved you from the ravages of sin—whether it was your own or someone else's? Have you ever thought of yourself as the object of God's unfailing love, mercy, and faithfulness? If you have read this book, you can be sure that you are the recipient of God's *chesed*—loved and chosen by God before time began. The details of your life are different than mine, but God's love and mercy are the same for you.

Consider the most famous verse of the Bible—John 3:16. I'm going to share it with you in a literal translation of the original Greek words:

> For God so loved the world that He gave His only begotten Son, that everyone believing *into* Him should not perish, but have everlasting life.[11]

When you repent of your sin and believe that Jesus died as your personal Substitute on the cross and rose from the dead, you believe *into* Jesus and into the new covenant with God. You leave your old identity behind and take up a new identity in Him. "Therefore, if anyone is in Christ, he is a new creation; old things have passed away; behold, all things have become new" (2 Cor. 5:17). God relates to you—the believer—as He relates to Jesus Christ. God loves *you* as He loves Jesus Christ (John 17:23).

Think of it this way: Jesus once said, "I am the door" (John 10:9). On one side of the door, we're filthy and burdened down with all our sin. We're ashamed before God because we bear the likeness of evil. Then, we walk through the door. Suddenly, we're sparkling clean! The burden is gone! Whether we realize it or not, in God's eyes we now bear the likeness of Jesus Christ, the

Chapter Eight

Holy Son of God. We are *in* Him! And going through the door is only the beginning of a brand new life *with* Him—a life with God through eternity! It's a life in which we come to know Him as much more than the door. He's everything we need.

You don't have to understand it all to begin. Just start. Trust God to lead you. Tell Him you want to believe into Jesus and receive the Holy Spirit. Ask Him to forgive your sins and cleanse you. Tell Him you want to give up your old life and receive His new life. Ask Him to help you understand more and more each day. Then allow Him to prepare your heart and mind for healing and change by reading and meditating on His word.

The kind of meditating Jesus wants you to do is not the same as I used to do when I followed the guru. When the Bible speaks of meditation, God means that He wants you to think about His word, ponder it, mutter it to yourself, speak it out loud, and let it sink into the deepest part of your heart. He wants you to believe all of His promises belong to you—promises for hope and a future as His beloved child. And because of Jesus' blood, even His commands become promises—that He will empower you to obey and be blessed.

Get to know God by spending time with Him. Talk to Him as you would your best friend, whether out loud or silently in your heart. Each time God shows you a part of your life that needs to be surrendered to Him, just do it, knowing that He'll replace it with something much better. He will withhold nothing good from those who walk uprightly. He says, "Open wide, and I will fill you."[12] He will give you the comfort, guidance, joy—and freedom—you have always longed for.

Believe Him. Believe His word—because when you do, you'll begin to see good changes in your life, whether your outward circumstances change or not. He will do this for you because He is the one and only Heart-Changer.

Conclusion

~ ~ ~

"Don't let anyone deceive you!"

Have you just begun your new life with God? Perhaps you've not yet believed into Jesus, but want to know more. Maybe you received Jesus as your Savior long ago, but you've never taken the time to get to know Him. In any case, rely on the Bible as your source of truth.

Just days before Jesus went to the cross, He gave His disciples a clear warning: "Watch out! Don't let anyone deceive you" (Matt. 24:3). He told them false prophets and false christs will do miraculous signs and wonders to deceive many people. Jesus warned that false teachers' lies will be so convincing that even the people God chose from eternity past could be fooled, if that were possible (Matt. 24:4-5, 11, 24).

Jesus' warning came just after He had spoken some very heated words to false teachers of a different sort. These men thought they were experts on the Scriptures, but they missed God's point altogether. They failed to believe that God's word applied to their own hearts, so they went around using it to condemn others while justifying themselves. They twisted the meaning of God's word so much that they didn't even recognize who Jesus was—the love of God in human flesh, proclaiming God's truth in front of their eyes.

There are many kinds of false teachers in the world today. Some tell lies about Jesus but seem believable because they do supernatural signs. Others twist God's word for their own purposes and deny that God still does miracles. Some, who seem to know a lot about the Bible, constantly spew out rules to follow and things to do to earn God's acceptance—but they all miss the whole point: God's grace.

How can you make sure you don't miss the point? How can you heed Jesus' warning—"Don't let anyone deceive you"? How can you be confident that you are following the way that will lead to eternal life with God, and to real and lasting heart-change? Most importantly, how can you know who Jesus really is? Jesus gives us the answer.

The night before He was crucified, Jesus prayed for His followers—not just the twelve disciples, but everyone who would ever believe in Him. This is what He asked God the Father to do for us: "Sanctify them by Your truth. Your word is truth" (John 17:17).

To sanctify us means to make us holy—to change us. It means to purify us and make us free from sin—to take us from who we've been to who God wants us to be. It means to make us more and more like Jesus.

And how did Jesus say this would happen? By God's truth—His word is truth. Only God's word, brought to life in your heart by His Spirit, can help you recognize the lies you've believed—about yourself, about your life, and about God. These lies have led to your emotional scars that trigger the feeling of lack and lead to sin. Only God's word and Spirit can overcome the effects these lies have had in your life so God can change you—and free you.

Give God a chance to prove Himself in your life. Ask Him to show you the truth. Ask Him to help you understand the Bible more than ever before. Then, dig in! Enter God's intensive care! Allow Him to get to the depths of your heart, your core beliefs, and every thought you have. Yes, it takes time. It also takes prayer, trust, and surrender. It takes your willingness to start and stick with it.

I humbly offer the Bible study in the following pages to help you get started. It contains some of the truths God has shown

Conclusion

me while in His intensive care. I join with you in this prayer as you begin:

Father in heaven, thank You for Your word. Thank You for giving us Your truth and sending Your Spirit as our teacher. I pray that You will open up Your word to me. Show me Your love. Shine Your light into the dark corners of my heart and expose the lies I've believed. Replace them with Your truth, and change me. Change my heart. Transform me into who you want me to be. In Jesus' name, amen.

The Bible: From Beginning to End, It's All About Jesus

I. The Beginning

- Read Genesis chapters 1 through 3.

God created the world as a place without sorrow or death. What changed all that?

Eve believed the lie, and both Adam and Eve acted on the lie. When Adam sinned, deceit entered the human heart. Human beings always speak and act out what is in their hearts. (Read Jesus' words in Matthew 15:18-19 and Luke 6:45.) Adam and Eve tried to hide—a form of deceit—and lies began pouring out of their mouths. Instead of admitting they had sinned, they tried to shift the blame.

- Read 1 John 3:21.
  When our hearts do not condemn us (pronounce us guilty and sentence us to death), we have confidence toward God. Did Adam and Eve have confidence to come into God's presence after they'd sinned?
  What does this say about their hearts?
  Based on these readings, what would you say is mankind's biggest problem?
- Read Jeremiah 17:9-10.

How does God describe the human heart?
Can we know our own hearts?
On whom can we rely to tell us the truth about our hearts?
- Read Hebrews 4:12.
  What does God use to show us the thoughts and intents of our hearts?
- Read Psalm 51:6.
  Does God want deceit (lies) in our hearts?
  What does He want in our "inner parts" instead?
  What does this verse say about wisdom?
- Read Psalm 119:9-11.
  What can we do to cleanse our way and to keep from sin? (How can we become wise?)

Our hearts are so deceitful that we are more willing to believe lies than the truth unless God helps us. Thankfully, He has helped us by giving us His word. Are you ready to look into God's word to find the truth about Jesus? Here we go!

II. Prophecy, Love, and the Cure for the Human Heart

God created mankind to have a close, intimate relationship with each one of us, but sin changed our hearts. Left on our own, we run from God instead of to Him. Sin ruined our relationship with God, and only He could fix it.

- Read Genesis 3:15.
  "And I will put enmity between you and the woman, and between your seed and her Seed; He shall bruise your head, and you shall bruise His heel."

God began to announce His cure for the human heart right there in the Garden of Eden, at the "scene of the crime." God declared that the Seed of the woman would crush the serpent's head—the cunning head of Satan, the deceiver. This Seed would be born as the product of woman, but not of man. God said that the serpent would bruise this Seed's heel, but, in doing so, the deceiver himself would be destroyed.

How could mankind recognize God's cure for the human heart—Jesus Christ, born of a virgin, crucified, and resurrected from the dead—from this single announcement? It would be impossible, or at least subject to legitimate debate. If God came in human flesh to fulfill His plan without explaining the reasons and details in advance, mankind could very well miss His coming and the point of it all. Or, if God didn't provide clear explanations in advance, His people could be deceived into believing a counterfeit.

Because of God's tremendous love for mankind, He greatly desired that we know His plan so we wouldn't miss it. So, for centuries, God revealed the details of His plan in advance—through object lessons, through living pictures that foreshadowed Jesus, and through the words of prophets. These "explanations in advance" are found throughout the Bible and are called prophecies. They provide the "who, what, when, where, why, and how" of God's plan. There are so many of these prophecies, it would be impossible for this book to mention all of them in detail, but let's look at a few.

The first time God mentions "love" in His Scriptures tells us a lot about how He loves us. Love is mentioned first in a scene that involves Abraham and his son of promise, Isaac.

Abraham waited many years for the son God promised. Isaac was a living miracle, born when Abraham was one hundred years old and his wife, Sarah, was ninety. God promised Abraham that the Messiah would come through Isaac's descendants (Genesis 12:1-3; 15:4-6; 17:19). But when Isaac was a young man, God tested Abraham with a command that seemed contradictory to His promise.

- Read Genesis 22:1-14.

What did God tell Abraham to do?
Did Abraham delay, or did he obey?
How close did Abraham come to sacrificing Isaac?
Who stopped him?
- Read Hebrews 11:17-19.
What did Abraham believe?
- Read Genesis 22:15-18.
What did the Lord promise Abraham and why?
What does God say about love in Genesis 22?

Focusing for a moment on Abraham's love, this scene shows that God knew Abraham loved Him supremely because Abraham obeyed His command. Abraham was willing to sacrifice Isaac, the son he loved. But Abraham could do this only because he knew God's love for him! Abraham knew that God's intentions toward him were good and that God is faithful to His promises. God's love was the source of Abraham's hope and strength, and it alone enabled Abraham to love and obey God above all.

Why is it important for you to know how deeply God loves you?

Now, go back and read Genesis 22:8 and 14 again. Who did Abraham say would provide the sacrifice? Where did Abraham say the sacrifice would be provided?

God used this event to show his great love for mankind. This scene in Abraham's life was a picture, a foreshadowing, of what God planned to do. It is one of God's "explanations in advance." Two thousand years later, God did provide Himself a Lamb. Jesus, God in human flesh—expressed in human language as God's beloved, only-begotten Son—became the Lamb who was sacrificed for our sin. Mount Moriah had become the site of the temple in Jerusalem, and it was outside the walls there that Jesus Christ was crucified as our substitute—just as the ram was Isaac's substitute. (Read the accounts of Jesus' crucifixion and resurrection in Matthew 26-28; Mark 14-16; Luke 22-24; and John 18-20.)

- Read Revelation 13:8 and John 1:29, 36.
  What do these verses say about who Jesus is?
  Genesis was written around 1400 B. C., and Revelation around 95 A. D. Based on these readings, can you see how God gave mankind a preview of how Jesus would die as our Substitute?

III. The Passover Lamb

- Read Genesis 15:13-14.
  What did God tell Abraham (then known as Abram) would happen to his descendants?
  How long would Abraham's descendants be strangers and servants in a foreign nation?
  What did God say He would do to that nation?

As time passed, God made His plan known to mankind in ways that were more and more obvious, using the descendants of Abraham to get His point across. God confirmed all His promises to Abraham with Isaac, and then with Isaac's son, Jacob—whose name God changed to Israel. Israel's family went to Egypt to escape a famine, and God sustained them there. But later Egypt became a place of bondage.

- Read Exodus 1:1-14.
  Why did the new king of Egypt (the Pharaoh) become afraid of the children of Israel?
  What did this king do to the children of Israel?

Pharaoh became so afraid of the children of Israel (the Hebrews) that making them slaves wasn't enough. He made a law requiring all male babies born to Hebrew women to be killed at birth. In this dangerous setting, Moses was born, but his parents weren't willing to let him be killed. His mother hid him, and

Pharaoh's daughter found him and adopted him as her own son. Moses grew up as Pharaoh's grandson. (Read about it in Exodus 1:15-2:10.)

As an adult, Moses made a choice. He left the luxuries of Pharaoh's household and gave up the riches and privileges available to him. (Read Hebrews 11:24-27.) Moses chose to be identified with his people in their affliction, and he was God's chosen man to deliver the Hebrews from slavery.

- Read Philippians 2:5-11; 2 Corinthians 8:9.

Based on these verses, how did Moses' decision give us a preview of what Jesus would do?

At the age of forty, Moses left Egypt hastily because he had killed an Egyptian for beating a Hebrew slave. Moses spent forty years in the desert tending sheep. Then, the Angel of the Lord appeared to him in an unusual display—a burning bush that was not consumed by the fire—and instructed him to return to Egypt to lead the Hebrews out of slavery. Moses went back to Egypt, but Pharaoh refused to allow the Hebrews to go despite a series of plagues with which God struck Egypt. (Read Exodus 2:11-10:29.)

The last plague was to be the death of all firstborn in the land of Egypt. Every firstborn child of every family, and even the firstborn of every animal, would die. God had a way to spare the Hebrews from this plague, and He gave Moses detailed instructions. Each Hebrew household was to choose a perfect, one-year-old male lamb on the tenth day of the first month and keep it under observation until the fourteenth day. During the four days, they were to make sure the lamb was perfect in every way. On the fourteenth day, they were to kill it at twilight. They were to sprinkle the lamb's blood on the two doorposts and lintel, then roast the lamb and eat it without breaking any of its bones. Each family would eat their roasted lamb that night, partaking in the sacrifice that provided the blood for their homes. This was the Lord's Passover. As the plague of death spread throughout every home in Egypt that night, the houses marked by the blood of a lamb were spared. (Read Exodus 12.)

This final plague convinced Pharaoh that he should let the Hebrews go free. God commanded them to observe Passover at the same time each year as a remembrance of their deliverance. But Passover was more than a remembrance. It was one of God's explanations in advance.

Many centuries later, Jesus became the ultimate Passover Lamb. He rode into Jerusalem as crowds shouted, "Be gracious and save us, Son of David! Blessed is He who comes in the name of the Lord! Hosanna in the highest!" (Matt. 21:9, author's paraphrase). With this greeting, the people "chose" Jesus, in that they recognized Him as their Messiah. For days, the religious leaders "inspected" Jesus for flaws. They interrogated Him while He taught in the temple. They tried to find some fault or sin in Him, but they couldn't. Nevertheless, they arrested Jesus and put Him on trial for saying that He was the Son of God. Pontius Pilate, the Roman governor, questioned Jesus and said, "I find no fault with this Man." Because the religious leaders insisted, Pilate ordered Jesus to be crucified. On the cross, Jesus gave up His life at Passover. The Roman executioners broke the legs of two thieves crucified at the same time as Jesus, but they didn't break any of His bones. The blood pouring from the wounds in Jesus' head and hands made the same pattern on the cross as the blood of the Passover lambs made on the doorposts and lintels centuries before.

The blood of the original Passover lambs kept out the plague of death and led to the Hebrews' freedom from slavery. The blood of the true Passover Lamb keeps us from the plague of eternal death and frees us from our slavery to sin!

- Read John 18:28-19:37.
- Read Colossians 1:13-14.
- Read 1 Corinthians 5:7-8.

Is Jesus Christ *your* Passover Lamb?

IV. The Veil Is Torn

After Moses led the children of Israel out of Egypt, God gave further instructions for other special times in addition to Passover. One of these special times, the Day of Atonement, is the "explanation in advance" that most clearly points to why Jesus is the only way to the presence of God.

The basic and most important instruction God gave to the children of Israel as they came out of Egypt was that they were to have no other gods. They were to worship the only true and living God, and only in the way He prescribed. God told Moses how to construct the tabernacle as the place where God's presence would dwell among them.

The tabernacle was separated into two sections—the Holy Place and the Most Holy Place—by a thick "veil." Inside the Most Holy Place was the Ark of the Covenant, a gold-overlaid box which contained God's commandments written on stone tablets. The Ark was covered by the mercy seat, and above the mercy seat the manifest presence of God dwelled in a bright light. (See, Exodus 25:10-22 and 26:31-34.)

Any Jewish priest could go into the Holy Place on any day, but they couldn't go past the veil into the Most Holy Place into the presence of God. Only one man, the high priest, could enter the Most Holy Place, and he only one day a year—on the Day of Atonement. On this one day of the year, he alone entered the Most Holy Place, into the presence of God, to make atonement for their sins. But he had to enter with blood.

First the high priest offered a young bull to make atonement for his sins, because it is the blood that makes atonement for the soul (Leviticus 17:11). The high priest went behind the veil and sprinkled some of the bull's blood on the mercy seat to cover his sins of the past year. Then he came out to sacrifice a goat. He went behind the veil again with the goat's blood and sprinkled it on the mercy seat to cover the people's sins for the year. (See, Leviticus 16:11-19.)

Why did God make these people go to such trouble to enter His presence? God was emphasizing at least four things. First, He is holy, and sin cannot enter His presence. Second, the consequence of sin is death. Third, life is in the blood, so the covering of sin requires shedding the blood of an innocent sacrifice. And fourth, He would allow a substitute sacrifice for the men and women He loved so dearly.

- Read Romans 3:23.
  How many people have sinned? So, how many need a blood sacrifice to enter God's presence?
- Read Hebrews 10:1-4.
  Could the animals' blood take away the people's sins? If animal sacrifices couldn't take away sins in the past, they can't today!

The Day of Atonement pointed forward to the ultimate Sacrifice who took away sins forever. Jesus was this innocent Sacrifice. He lived in sinless obedience because God's love, not deceit, was in His heart. He came to offer His body—flesh and blood—for the sin of mankind. His blood paid the price for sin, once for all. (Read Hebrews 7:27, 9:12, and 10:10.) But there's more.

- Read Matthew 27:45-51.

The Day of Atonement was originally observed in the tabernacle, which was a special large tent that could be taken down and moved as the children of Israel journeyed through the wilderness. In later years, the tabernacle was replaced by a permanent temple in Jerusalem. A magnificent structure, the temple was constructed according to the same design as the tabernacle, with the Holy Place and the Most Holy Place. The

Most Holy Place was separated by a veil. This veil was not some flimsy, see-through material. It was woven from many cloths and was about five inches thick and sixty feet high. When Jesus died on the cross, the veil was torn—literally ripped in two from top to bottom. No human hands could have done it. God tore the veil because the sacrifice of Jesus, our Substitute, opened the way to His holy presence. Because of Jesus' blood, the way to God is open—to those who receive Jesus as Savior.

- Read Hebrews 9:23-26.

God had given Moses the design for the tabernacle, and thus for the temple as well. They were patterned after God's temple in heaven. After Jesus' sacrifice, He Himself took His own blood into the real Most Holy Place—the Holiest of Holies in heaven. According to Hebrews 9:24, for whom did Jesus do this?

- Read Hebrews 10:5-22.
- Read Hebrews 4:14-16.

Does the blood of Jesus make it possible for you to run to God's presence to find help every time you need it?

V. Faith Replaces Fear

After the children of Israel had left Egypt, they came to the wilderness around Mount Sinai. Moses went up on the mountain to receive God's instructions. God said to tell the people that He would manifest His presence there, in their sight, in three days. The people made preparations, but when God's presence came, they were frightened, not comforted. God manifested His presence on Mount Sinai in fire. The whole mountain quaked and was completely covered in smoke. A long and loud trumpet blast heralded God's presence, attesting to His majesty and holiness.

- Read Exodus 19.

The children of Israel, like all other human beings, had hearts infected with sin and deceit. Just like Adam and Eve, they wanted to hide from the presence of God. They couldn't literally hide behind trees in the wilderness, but they essentially hid their hearts.

- Read Exodus 20:18-19.
  Did the children of Israel want to speak to God directly?
  What did they fear would happen if they did?

The people feared death from the very Source of life! They had forgotten that God was not the author of death; it came as a result of Adam's sin. Like Adam and Eve, the people had no faith in God's goodness toward them. But Moses pleaded with them.

- Read Exodus 20:20.

Moses' plea may seem a bit confusing until one understands his original words in Hebrew. When he first said, "Do not *fear*," he used the word "yare," which means to be frightened or afraid. But when he said, "that His *fear* may be before you," Moses used the word "yirah." In Hebrew, the difference between these two words is that, in the latter, there is an added ה or "he," pronounced "hay." This is the fifth letter of the Hebrew alphabet, and it symbolizes God's grace. God wanted to breathe grace into the fear of the people, for "yirah" means "reverential fear that acknowledges God's good intentions."[13]

God wanted to do good for the children of Israel, but their hearts were so clouded by sin and deceit that, as a whole, they couldn't see His good intentions. They were afraid and unwilling to enjoy the intimacy of knowing Him.

- Read Hebrews 11:6.
  How is it possible to please God?
  What two things does a person of faith believe about God?
  Do you believe God will reward you if you seek Him with all your heart?
- Read 1 John 1:7-9.
  Will God cleanse you from all sin and unrighteousness?
  Does Jesus' blood cleanse you from all sin?

Because God wanted a relationship with people who were not frightened away by fear, He promised to manifest Himself in a different way.

- Read Deuteronomy 18:15-19.
  Whom did God promise to send?
  Do you think it is easier to approach God knowing that He has come to us as one of us, as a human being?
- Read Luke 24:19; John 6:14; John 17:8; Acts 3:22-26.

Who is the Prophet God sent?

VI. The Messiah Had to Suffer

God gave one of the most important "explanations in advance" around 700 B.C. through Isaiah the prophet.

- Read Isaiah 53.

God was pleased to send Jesus to be wounded for our transgressions and bruised for our iniquities. Jesus' suffering was God's own offering for our sin. Read Matthew 26:47 through 27:51 to see how the prophecies of Isaiah were fulfilled in Jesus' suffering.

- Was Jesus despised and rejected by men?
- Did Jesus keep silent when He was accused?
- Did the Roman soldier give Jesus "stripes" on His back by scourging Him with a whip?
- Did a rich man bury Jesus in a tomb?
- Read Zechariah 11:12-13; Psalm 22; Psalm 69:20-21. Were these prophecies fulfilled in Jesus' suffering and death?
- Read Luke 24:25-27, 44-47. What did Jesus say about His suffering and death?

VII. God's Timetable

So far in our study, we've seen the "who," "what," and "how" of God's explanations in advance, or prophecies. Clearly, these prophecies point to Jesus, who would come into this world to make it possible for human beings to live in the close, intimate relationship with God for which they'd been created. Jesus had to do everything necessary to change our hearts so that we can run to God in faith, not run from Him in fear. Jesus had to suffer the death that our sins demanded. He would be whipped to shreds, beaten, and nailed to a cross, shedding His blood to make us right with God.

Now we turn to "when." Did God actually tell His people in advance when they could expect the Messiah? Yes, He did, through a prophet named Daniel. This particular "explanation in advance" involves a lot of history, so hang on.

- Read Daniel 9:24-27.

Daniel was a descendant of Abraham who lived during a time of God's judgment upon His people for centuries of ignoring Him and worshiping other gods. The Babylonian army destroyed Jerusalem, and God caused His people to be taken into captivity in Babylon for seventy years. Daniel was one of the first to be taken, and even though he was essentially a slave in a foreign land where everyone worshiped other gods, he lived a life of obedience and faithfulness to the true and living God. He was an old man when God gave him this prophecy.

To understand the prophecy, one must understand how God's people counted time. Ever since God gave the law to Moses as the children of Israel came out of Egypt, they were to count time in seven year cycles, or "weeks" of years. For six years the people were to farm the land and harvest their crops, but the seventh year was to be a Sabbath of rest for the land. Each seven year period constituted a "week," also known as a Sabbatical cycle.

At the time of Daniel's prophecy, God determined a total of seventy weeks, or Sabbatical cycles, for the children of Israel and Jerusalem. These seventy cycles would be divided into sections. There would be a period of seven Sabbatical cycles, then another period of sixty-two. These sixty-nine weeks, or 483 years, would cover the time between the command to rebuild Jerusalem until the time of the Messiah, who would be "cut off"—put to death—but not for Himself (for sinful humankind).

The timetable began when the seventy year captivity ended, and Daniel was alive to see the event that triggered the first period of seven Sabbatical cycles. Babylon was conquered by the Medo-Persians, and the new Persian king, Cyrus, gave the decree for the Jews to return to Jerusalem to rebuild the temple in 536 B.C. By September 535 B.C., over 49,000 Jews had returned to Jerusalem. The captivity had officially ended. The first seven Sabbatical cycles began the next year.

Seven cycles passed, ending in 485 B.C., during the ministry of the prophet Zechariah. God stopped speaking through his prophets after Zechariah until Malachi—who ministered during the Sabbatical cycles covering 436 to 422 B.C. Thus, there was a gap of time between the end of the first seven cycles and the beginning of the sixty-two Sabbatical cycles. Malachi was the last prophet of "the Prophets." God's speaking through him began the next period of sixty-two Sabbatical cycles—a period of 434 years, which ended in 2 B.C., the year of Jesus' birth. The last words of Malachi's prophecy indicate the link to the time of the Messiah's birth.

- Read Malachi 4:5-6.
- Read Luke 1 and 2.

John the Baptist, who was born six months before Jesus, fulfilled Malachi's prophecy about Elijah coming to turn the hearts of the fathers and their children. John wasn't a reincarnation of Elijah. Elijah never died. (Read 2 Kings 2:4-11.) John the Baptist came in the spirit and power of Elijah.

How did John turn the hearts of the fathers and children? He didn't preach about sacrifices to atone for sin under the Law of Moses. No, he preached about repentance—hearts turning from sin back to God. John prepared his followers' hearts for the truth by recognizing that external religious acts, such as sacrifices, could never save their deceitful sin-infected hearts. Mankind needs a Savior, One who can truly change human hearts.

- Read Matthew 4:17 and Mark 1:15.
  What did Jesus tell people to do?
- Read Matthew chapter 5 through chapter 7.

Jesus taught that God's law goes much deeper than outward actions. Murder is deeper than the act of taking another's life; murder is in the heart of a person who is angry without a cause. Adultery is deeper than cheating on a spouse; it's in the heart of anyone looking around with lustful thoughts. And idolatry is much deeper than bowing down to other gods; it's in our hearts when we are dissatisfied with what God has provided for us. God's commandments were meant to go beyond outward actions into our hearts—to expose the lack of love towards God and other human beings. But God's commandments alone have no power to help us obey. When we believe into Jesus, we receive a new heart that wants to obey and the Holy Spirit to empower us.

VIII. Where?

Jesus arrived exactly as God had foretold through the prophets. God had even told "where" in advance—where He'd be born, where He would travel, and where He would live and minister.

- Read Micah 5:2; Hosea 11:1; Matthew 2:1-23; Isaiah 9:1-2; Matthew 4:12-17.

IX. But why?

God manifested Himself in human flesh—as a Man, a Prophet like Moses, so as not to frighten us, but to draw us to Himself. Jesus was fully God, yet fully human. As the Seed of the woman, He was born of a virgin by the power of the Holy Spirit. As a man, He was tempted in all ways as we are, but He did not sin. He never acted independently of His Father's will. Every word Jesus said and every act He did was in loving obedience to the Father. Through His perfect obedience to the will of God, Jesus attained the perfection Adam did not. By His sacrificial death and resurrection, Jesus defeated Satan just as God foretold in the Garden of Eden. It is only a matter of time before Satan is removed from the earth and Jesus sets up His everlasting kingdom (Revelation 20-22).

We've looked at God's "explanations in advance" that explain "who, what, when, where, and how." But *why* did God do all this for us? His word is clear.

- Read John 15:13-17.
- Read 1 John 4:9-19.

- Read John 3:16-21.
- Read Romans 8:29-39.
- Read Ephesians 1:3-12; 3:10-12.

The answer is clear. Do you know this answer in your heart? Do you believe it applies to you? It does! Believe it: Jesus loves you! It doesn't matter if you can't feel it yet. Just believe it and begin thanking God for His love.

X. Where is Jesus Now?

- Read Acts 1:1-11.
- Read Acts 3:19-21.
- Read Acts 7, especially verses 55-56.
- Read Ephesians 1:15-23.
  Where is Jesus now?
- Read Hebrews 7:25; 1 John 2:1
  What is Jesus doing for us while He is at the Father's right hand?

XI. Will Jesus Return?

In Daniel's prophecy, God said there would be seventy "weeks," or Sabbatical cycles, in His timetable, but so far we've covered only sixty-nine of them. The seventieth week hasn't happened yet. Remember the gap in God's timetable between the prophets Zechariah and Malachi? We are now in another gap in God's timetable, a time in which the truth about Jesus is being preached all over the world and people are being saved. But this gap won't last forever. The seventieth week will be the last seven years before Jesus returns to set up His kingdom on the earth. (God's timetable according to Daniel's prophecy will begin to run again when a powerful world leader confirms a seven-year treaty with the people of Israel. At the same time, God will send two prophets as witnesses to His truth. You can read about them in Revelation 11:3-13. These prophets will most likely be the two men who have not yet died—Enoch and Elijah. (See, Gen. 5:21-24 and 2 Kings 2:4-11.) So, just as the first gap in Daniel's timetable coincided with the years between Zechariah and Malachi, this final gap is the time between Jesus and these two prophets.)

- Read Matthew 24:29-31.
- Read John 14:2-3.
- Read Acts 1:9-11.
- Read Revelation 22:20.

There are hundreds of prophecies about Jesus throughout the Bible—from beginning to end. Many of them were fulfilled in Jesus' first coming, and the rest will be fulfilled when He comes again to set up God's kingdom on earth.

- Read Matthew 24:36.
- Read Acts 1:6-7.
  Who did Jesus say knows when He will return?
- Read Matthew 25:31-46.
- Read Matthew 28:16-20.
- Read Mark 16:14-20.
- Read Titus 2:11-14.
  What does Jesus want us to do until He returns?
- Read Romans 5:6-11.
- Read Romans 8:31-39.
- Read Hebrews 13:5-6.
  What does God want us always to remember about His love?

XII. What is Jesus saying to you?

Then Jesus said, "Come to me, all of you who are weary and carry heavy burdens, and I will give you rest. Take my yoke upon you. Let me teach you, because I am humble and gentle at heart, and you will find rest for your souls. For my yoke is easy to bear, and the burden I give you is light" (Matt. 11:28-30 NLT).

Now, what will you say to Him?

Jesus,
I believe You are the Son of God and You came to earth in human flesh.
I believe that You died on the cross for my sins.
I believe You gave Your life-blood so that I can be cleansed and have a relationship with God, now and forever.
I believe You rose from the dead, in victory over sin and death, to give me new life.
I receive Your cleansing and forgiveness, and I now forgive those who have hurt me.
Thank You for the gift of a relationship with God.
I believe God accepts me, and does not reject me, because of You, Jesus.
I give up my old life of sin and obedience to Satan.
I receive Your life of victory over sin. I am born again.
Set me completely free.
God, fill me with Your Holy Spirit. Teach me Your ways. Change my heart.
Teach me how to let Your love pour through me.
Teach me how to surrender all to You.
Let Your word come alive in my heart and help me apply it to my life.
Make me into all You want me to be.
Amen!

Endnotes

Chapter 4
1. *Chesed* is a Hebrew word pronounced "hess-ed," but with the "h" spoken deep in the throat.
2. "The Solid Rock," by Edward Mote (1797-1874). William B. Bradbury (1816-1868) wrote the music.

Chapter 5
3. "There is a Redeemer," by Melody Green, copyright Birdwing Music/Cherry Lane Music Publishing Co., Inc. (1982).
4. Years later, I found ample ethnological and linguistic evidence that supports the Bible's account of creation. See, Kang and Nelson, *The Discovery of Genesis: How the Truths of Genesis Were Found Hidden in the Chinese Language*, Concordia Publishing House, St. Louis, Missouri, 1979; Nelson and Broadberry, *Genesis and the Mystery Confucius Couldn't Solve*, Concordia Publishing House, St. Louis, Missouri, 1994; Olson, *Bruchko*, Creation House (New Wine Press, Chichester, England), 1978; Richardson, *Eternity in Their Hearts*, Regal Books, Ventura, California, 1984.

Chapter 6
5. The text summarizes some aspects of Genesis chapters one through three; however, it would be

beneficial to read these chapters for yourself at this point.

Chapter 7

6. "There is a River," words and music by Jessie Rogers ©2002 Music Missions Publishing/ASCAP.
7. Andrew Murray, *The Master's Indwelling*, Whitaker House, New Kensington, PA (1983) (page 194, used by permission).
8. The information on the brain and neurotransmitters in these paragraphs is based on NIDA's "Drugs, Brains, and Behavior: The Science of Addiction," NIH Publ. No. 10-5605 (public domain). See also, http://learn.genetics.utah.edu/content/addiction.
9. See, "General Chemistry Online: The Bliss Molecule," at http://antoine.frostburg.edu/chem/sense/101/features/anadamide.shtml. Copyright 1997-2010 by Fred Senese.

Chapter 8

10. Malcolm Smith, *The Power of the Blood Covenant*, Harrison House, Tulsa, 2002.
11. John 3:16, *The Interlinear Greek-English New Testament, Third Edition*, Ed. Jay P. Green, Sr., Baker Books, Grand Rapids, 1996, and *A Literal Translation of the Holy Bible*, Jay P. Green, Sr. , 1996 (emphasis added).
12. See, Psalm 84:10 and 81:10.

Conclusion

13. See "yare," #3373; and, "yirah," #3374. *The Complete Word Study Dictionary Old Testament*, Dr. Warren Baker and Dr. Eugene Carpenter, AMG Publishers, Chattanooga, 2003.

CPSIA information can be obtained at www.ICGtesting.com
Printed in the USA
BVOW071051030512

289282BV00003B/4/P

9 781449 736835